D0756484

GLEN ...st date stamped below.

GLENYS BARTON

Adrian Flowers   Robin Gibson
Edward Lucie-Smith

Foreword
Charles Saumarez Smith

Introduction
Robert Heller

momentum

ACKNOWLEDGEMENTS

Glenys Barton would like to thank:
Robert Heller for his eloquent introduction and his constant support as friend and collector. Edward Lucie-Smith, whose understanding of objects is supreme, for his critical biography and for his interest and criticism which has been a great support to her from the beginning of her career. Robin Gibson for his poetic appraisal of her portraits and for giving her so much quiet encouragement in the making of them. Howard Smith for his perceptive comments on his studio visits and for helping to make this book possible. Special thanks to Adrian Flowers for intuitive and beautiful photographs over the years. Finally a big thankyou to Sarah Howgate for being by her side, devoting the hours of patient attention necessary to produce this book and the two exhibitions.

With support from

NATIONAL
PORTRAIT
GALLERY

manchester city art galleries

All photography by Adrian Flowers with the exception of the following:-
Frank Thurston p.12, 14, 16, 17(top) Richard Davies p.18, 19, 20, 21, 22, 23, 24
Karen Norquay back cover, p.25, 29, 30, 32, 33, 68 Tim Hill p.35 Michael Walchover p.13, 15 Gareth Winters p.57, 89(top)

First published in Great Britain in 1997 by
Momentum, P.O. Box 12752, London E8 3UA

ISBN 1 873362 66 8 (paper)
ISBN 1 873362 67 6 (cased)

Designed by Peter Gladwin
Coordinated by Sarah Howgate

Typeset in Minion
Printed in London by The Pale Green Press

Glenys Barton is represented by Angela Flowers Gallery

Flowers East
199 – 205 Richmond Road
London E8 3NJ
Telephone 0181- 985 3333 Facsimile 0181- 985 0067

For Martin and Felix, Angela and Matthew

FOREWORD

At a time when many painters of talent and imagination think twice before undertaking a portrait, it is extremely encouraging to come across a creative personality from another discipline who has taken to portraiture with the enthusiasm and inventiveness of Glenys Barton. In a medium as old as civilisation, ceramic sculpture has acquired in Barton's hands new life and vigour, and she can now be seen to a considerable extent to have filled the void left in figurative sculpture in Britain since the death of Elisabeth Frink. Her bust of the late Jean Muir was one of those all too rare portraits which seem to encapsulate both all the essential characteristics of a well-known sitter and the spirit of the age in which it was created. Since it became the undoubted star of the National Portrait Gallery's *The Portrait Now* exhibition in 1993/4, the Gallery has had a special relationship with Glenys Barton, leading both to a successful commission for the portrait of Glenda Jackson MP, and to a retrospective exhibition of Barton's portraits which the Gallery is delighted to be holding in Autumn 1997. We are grateful both to the artist and to Matthew Flowers and Sarah Howgate of Flowers East for their assistance and enthusiastic support for the exhibition. We are also particularly pleased that Manchester City Art Galleries will be showing their exhibition of Glenys Barton's recent works at the same time as ours, and are grateful to Howard Smith for his cooperation on this venture. Both exhibitions will be appropriately shown together in Glenys Barton's home town of Stoke on Trent at the City Museum and Art Gallery from January to March 1998.

Charles Saumarez Smith
Director, National Portrait Gallery

LEFT:
Jean Muir (Detail)   **1992**

46 x 19 x 12 cms
Collection: Scottish National Portrait Gallery

INTRODUCTION
ROBERT HELLER

The so-called 'tendencies' in contemporary art rarely encourage today's practitioners to seek the clarity, purity and craftsmanship of the Renaissance tradition. Glenys Barton, with her pursuit of perfect form, and her passionate search among ceramic techniques for the matching means, is fully in that great tradition: her moving Madonnas, based on a famous Piero della Francesca image, bear eloquent witness to Barton's artistic provenance.

Yet she is also fully contemporary, not only in that restless search for new imagery and execution, but in the mood of her pieces, and much else besides. Whether the subject is her own body, or the heads of friends, or explorations of the feminine identity, or portraits of the famous, the work is always truly conceptual, always penetrates far behind the motif. Barton is deeply concerned with her times, and these enquiring, contemplative works beautifully express her philosophical as well as her artistic concerns.

The key word in that sentence is 'beautifully'. The beauty of Barton's successful pieces is inescapable. Beauty doesn't rank high among the attributes that artists seek today, or that critics applaud. Yet its dictionary definition, 'the quality that gives pleasure to the sight, or aesthetic pleasure generally', underlies the whole history and practice of painting and sculpture. Just how that quality of beauty is achieved, too, has profound importance. Barton's ability to exploit ceramics as her medium is inseparable from her broader objectives – and she is proficient to a degree.

The technique varies markedly: the swing between hand building and slip casting has been a profitable source of creative energy. Whatever method she uses, and whether the work is based on drawing or photography, the ultimate form is a constant concern. Her friend Jacqueline Poncelet has written about the 'endless discussions on the merits of accuracy' as Barton worked on slip cast heads of Jacqueline and her husband, the sculptor Richard Deacon – works which were not designed as portraits, but as essays in ceramic sculpture:

'The finished heads were extremely beautiful in their austerity, but bore very little resemblance to either of us as individuals, being as they were shaven-headed and without expression.'

LEFT:
Pink Madonna   1986

43 cms high
Private Collection, UK

Austere beauty is a characteristic of Barton's earlier work, whether the piece is white or tinted. Partly because of the characteristics of the ceramic material itself, a degree of austerity persists into the later heads, which are genuine and very recognisable likenesses. Indeed, Barton's ability to counterfeit the appearance of flesh, blood and bones is phenomenal. This is not imitation, but recreation, in which the artist combines psychological and physical insights in a profoundly moving manner.

As with all truly creative careers, however, the success of the later work does not diminish the power of its predecessors. Barton's career has continuously sought and achieved progress, both technical and artistic, while bringing each successive phase to convincing fruition. Experiment has become a crucial theme in Barton's artistic development; for example, her use first of stylisation, then of distortion, as she sought, slowly but steadily, to strengthen her means of expression.

Every experiment, however, has only confirmed Barton's place in the artistic lineage which stretches back in time, past the modern masters and the Cubist preoccupation with angles of vision, to the flowing aesthetics of the Renaissance and further back still to the elemental calm of Asian religious sculpture. Artists create their own language out of the phrases handed down from the past. Barton's evolving language has added to that lexicon, and future artists will be grateful for that. But Barton clearly has new riches in store – and the two excellent essays in this book show clearly the sources both of an admirable past and an exciting future.

RIGHT:
Two Faces   **1994**

25 x 28 x 21 cms

Graphic Permutations I No. 1   1972

Bone China
10.5 x 10.5 x 10.5 cms

GLENYS BARTON
by Edward Lucie-Smith

Speaking of her own work Glenys Barton quotes the curator and art-historian John Elderfield's comment on Matisse – that "he was working towards serenity by means of simplification". She adds: "This exactly describes what I would like to be doing."

Like that of many artists, her work falls into several distinct phases. Each of these, she points out, is connected with a particular working environment. From 1972–76, for example, Barton shared a cramped, rather dank little studio slotted into a railway arch behind St. Pancras station with her lifelong friend Jacqueline Poncelet. She had travelled a comparatively circuitous route in order to get there. Born in Stoke-on-Trent, the centre of the commercial ceramic industry in Britain, she comes from a working-class background. Her father was a miner, later disabled, who became a newsagent; her mother was a hand-painter on china; her aunts were gilders. She began her career by training to be a teacher in Bristol, though she nevertheless admits that even in those days she "did pottery all the time" and treated the training college as if it were an art school. At the same time, she did a lot of dance and movement – something which she now believes had a crucial impact on her early work.

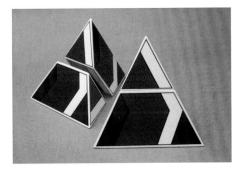

Pyramid I No. 2   1972

Bone China
11.5 cms high

After completing her training, she taught at Risinghill, a tough London comprehensive school. After eighteen months of this she had a nervous breakdown. After her recovery, she worked at the Institute of Education at London University as a potter's assistant.

The pots and drawings she was then making were seen, more or less by accident, by someone who worked at the Royal College of Art. She was encouraged to apply, and, after what she describes as "a stormy interview", was accepted, at the comparatively late age of twenty-five. It was, nevertheless, a propitious moment to begin a career as an artist – Pop Art was just coming to the end of its first and most important period of development; Minimal Art was gathering strength.

However, Glenys Barton did not at this moment believe that art would be her career. When she entered the RCA what she wanted to be was an industrial designer. At first she showed every sign of succeeding in this ambition. While still a student, she designed a range of domestic wares for Habitat, the department store founded by Terence Conran, which had pioneered a new set of attitudes towards the British domestic environment. This range was accepted and put into production – the fulfilment, as Barton herself has since remarked, of every ambitious student's dream.

Despite this, midway through her time at the RCA she became dissatisfied with what she was doing, and rebelled against the future she had so neatly mapped out. Trying to explain this change of heart, she once told me that she could not accept the compromises which a career in industrial design seemed to involve – both the perpetual concession to the profit motive and, worse still, the lack of imagination which seemed characteristic of the commercial manufacturers with whom she came into contact. What the college had given her was the thing which unfitted her for the career she had originally chosen: a head-on encounter with what she calls "the shock of art". Among those chiefly responsible for bringing this shock home to her, she cites Eduardo Paolozzi and the late Hans Coper, both of whom were attached to the ceramics department of the RCA at this time. She also feels a major debt of gratitude to David Queensbury who was then Professor.

Returning to the idea of purely individual work, she discovered, perhaps slightly to her horror, that it was impossible to go back to the point where she had left off when she decided to commit herself to industrial design. She had lost a certain sort of innocence: "After making precise models, I

Fifth Plane   1974

Bone China
30.5 x 30.5 x 7.5 cms

couldn't go back to using clay as I had used it before." Years ago, when I first knew her work, Barton described to me the excitement she felt when she first encountered switch boxes made of electro-porcelain. "Factory-made," she said, producing an example for me to look at, "and accurate to a thou." She then added: "Clay can be either soft or hard. I only discovered its hardness through industrial porcelain."

Essentially this discovery set the scene for the first phase of her career. There were other important and slightly unexpected elements as well. One factor was the dance-training she had had while she was still at college in Bristol:

> Dance was for a long time my most vivid artistic
> experience. It can be so spontaneously creative: the
> image and the feeling so close and controlled, one's own
> body diminutive, moving in a void. Studying Laban
> movement, an analysis of the moving figure in space;
> moments like 'Monotones' [choreographed by Frederick
> Ashton] danced by the Royal Ballet Company (stark
> black and white figures on a square of stage) helped to
> crystallise an awareness of our relationship with space
> and gave me an ambition to formalise it. [i]

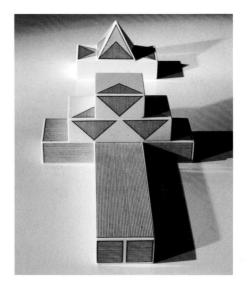

Untitled   1973

Bone China
5 x 5 x 2.5 cms

Other influences, dating from her Royal College of Art period, were both diverse and unexpected. One was Stanley Kubrick's film, '2001 – A Space Odyssey'. She was completely captivated by the mysterious monolith which plays such a prominent part in this, and also by the immaculate white moulded interiors of Kubrick's spaceships – "better than any sculpture I had ever seen":

> The last sequences of the film set me thinking about
> time and our suspension within it... while the final shots
> of the facsimile room haunted me like a Chirico
> landscape. [ii]

Less surprisingly, she was, like many young artists of her generation at the RCA, strongly attracted by American Minimal Art. 'The Art of the Real' exhibition at the Tate Gallery, exploring this new trend, had a great impact on her. She liked the 'direct, powerful simplicity' of these sculptural objects, but at the same time resisted Minimalism's tendency to leave things open-ended – to treat the pattern of absolute order as something which could best be completed by the spectator.

i   Glenys Barton, 'A Search for Order,' *Ceramic Review*, No. 34, 1975
ii   ibid

Yet another influence was the simplified architecture which was being created at the time – buildings like the black glass slab of the IBM headquarters in Portsmouth, or the solid yet elusive (because reflective) mass of Arne Jacobsen's Bank of Denmark in Copenhagen. In her own mind she compared these contemporary buildings to the visionary projects of the French neo-classical architects Boullée and Ledoux, who were at that moment becoming the objects of renewed scholarly attention. These neo-classicists, Barton felt, longed for extreme purity and simplicity, yet wanted to arouse emotion through the use of expressive forms. Here was something she could empathise with. Later, after a visit to Mexico, she was to feel a fascination with the brutal simplicity of Pre-Columbian temple architecture, and especially with the pyramidal temples in Mexico, with their steep flights of steps.

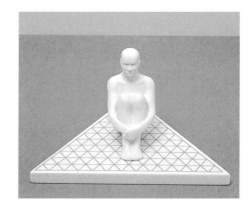

First Island   1974

Bone China
13.5 x 12 x 7 cms

Cloud Cubes   1970

Bone China
10 x 10 x 10 cms

At the same time, however, she had a very British reluctance to banish the human figure – a reluctance which was reinforced by her continuing fascination with the dance. Here a literary source came to her rescue – the early stories of J.G. Ballard, and in particular the short story 'Terminal Beach' in which a lone character, Travern, has trapped himself on a totally man-made island:

> I was so excited by Ballard's work that I based [a] series of sculptures on 'Terminal Beach' and another Ballard short story – 'Concrete Island'. After reading Ballard, words like zone, matrix, meridian, stratum, eclipse began to acquire new layers of meaning.[iii]

These were the sculptures Barton was making during her period in the St. Pancras studio – basically a most unpromising environment for such precise work. During this period she became identified, like a number of other British ceramic artists of the same generation, with the craft revival which was taking place at that time. She was included, for example, in the major survey show 'The Craftsman's Art', held at the Victoria & Albert Museum in 1973, and in 'Aspects of British Crafts', held at the Royal Scottish Museum in the same year.

Despite her participation in these exhibitions, the identification with craft is something which Barton has always resisted. She feels in fact that she has sometimes been disadvantaged, and ignored by critics, because she uses a material – clay – which is now automatically associated with the world of craft, even though her own practice has little to do with supposedly craft attitudes. She goes so far as to say that she has had to fight harder on this issue than on the issue of gender. "I want to emphasise," she says in a recent letter "that I never think about [gender] in relation to my work, unless someone else brings the subject up... I just want to be judged as an artist, not as a female one."[iv]

The thing which made this a practical ambition was her encounter with the dealer Angela Flowers in 1974. The two were introduced by Barton's fellow ceramist Carole McNicholl, whom she had met at the RCA. A two-person exhibition was suggested, but Angela Flowers said that, on principle, she only did one-person shows. Henceforth Barton was to be regarded, and treated, like any other artist in the gallery's stable. The materials she used were not an issue.

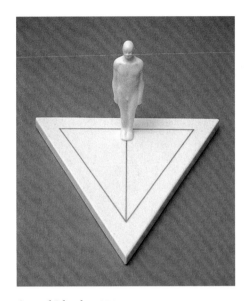

Second Island   1974

Bone China
13.5 x 8 x 12 cms

Advent   1974

Bone China
11.5 x 5 x 15 cms

iii   ibid.
iv   letter to the author, February 1997

Head with Relief Figures   1976/77

Bone China
17 cms high

RIGHT:

Prototype for Head with Relief Figures   1976/77

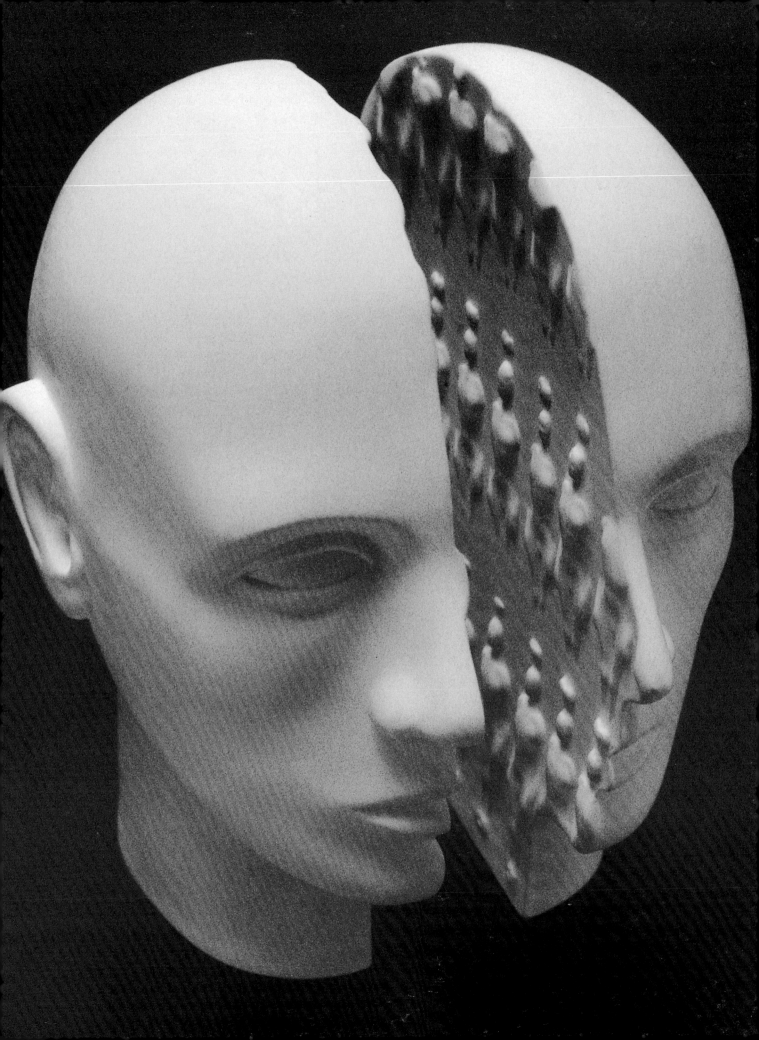

Sky Plateau 2   1976/77

Bone China
25 cms diameter

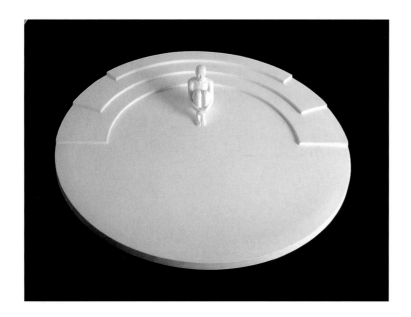

Arena   1977

Bone China
37.5 cms diameter

RIGHT:
Time at Yagul   1976/77

Bone China
17.5 cms high

The small-scale work in bone china which Barton made in the St. Pancras studio led directly to the next phase, which was her work with Wedgwood. The association was appropriate in two ways – first, because the firm of Wedgwood was intimately associated with the rise of the Neo-classical Movement in art, some aspects of which already fascinated the sculptor. Second, because the primary material at Wedgwood was bone china, which Barton was already used to handling. Nevertheless her arrival caused a certain amount of trepidation in the firm, as John Mallet, then Keeper of the Department of Ceramics at the Victoria & Albert Museum, later recorded in a catalogue essay.[v] Barton, too, had to struggle hard on her side to create a working relationship. Her over-riding concern was, as Mallet says, "to achieve the 'absolute perfection' of execution necessary to the execution of her vision."[vi]

The period at Wedgwood represented the culmination of Barton's experiments with refined, ultra-precise effects – it was the time when she most regularly achieved the foreseen, regular, predictable result which expressed a concept fully formed before the piece was ever modelled or went into the kiln. In a sense, as she discovered when she returned to independent work in London, it also amounted to a dead end.

The next phase was to be very different. She was now, after a brief period working in the front room of a house in Wandsworth, making use of a studio in Brixton borrowed from the sculptor Richard Deacon. This was a very different environment from the ones she had been accustomed to previously – large, ramshackle and not very clean. She was independent of the demands made by a large organisation with its own traditions and firmly established ways of working, and did not have to consider any needs other than her own. On the other hand, the condition of the studio made it very nearly impossible to achieve the clean purity of surface which she had regarded as desirable hitherto. Having decided that she needed to go in a new direction, she embraced the situation she now had, by actually building a primitive kiln in the studio yard in order to smoke her work.

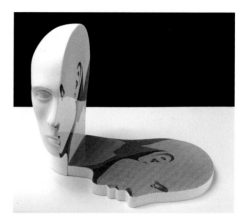

Jungian Shadow I   1976/77

Bone China
17 cms high

---

v   Edward Lucie-Smith and John Mallet, Glenys Barton at Wedgwood, Victoria & Albert Museum, London, 1977.
vi   Mallet in op. cit., p.12

Life Diagram I/II/II   1976/77

24.2 cms diameter

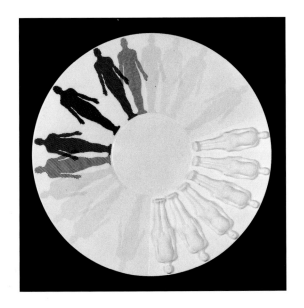

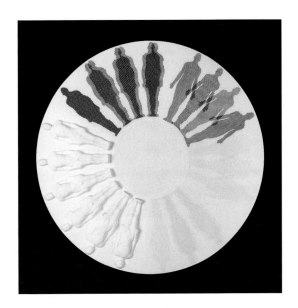

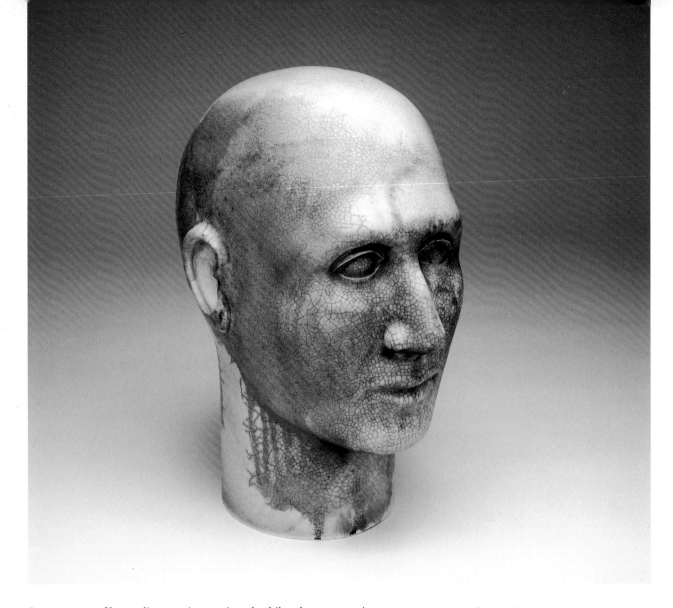

Some aspects of her earlier practice continued, while others were quite radically altered. For example, many of the pieces continued to be made in moulds, and the basic form was therefore just as carefully controlled as it had been previously. But this control was often contradicted not merely by the use of smoking, which produces random effects of colour, but by heavily crackled glazes. Barton was now teaching at Camberwell School of Art, and took the opportunity to learn more about glazes from Colin Pearson, who also taught there. A key piece from this period is the over-lifesize head *Ozymandias*, which dates from 1979. This marked a decisive step forward in her development. While the human figure had made previous appearances in her sculpture, it had tended to be small in scale, and linked to a carefully constructed setting. *Ozymandias* was life-size and completely independent. Barton has always been extremely conscious of possible historical precedents for her work. Her exemplars here seem to have been the so-called 'reserve heads' found in certain Ancient Egyptian tombs of the Old Kingdom period.

Ozymandias 1979

45.5 cms high

LEFT:
Monte Alban 1976/77

Bone China
39.5 cms high

After using Deacon's studio for about a year, Glenys Barton moved to a studio of her own in Barmouth Road, Wandsworth. She occupied this from 1980–84. At the Barmouth Road studio she continued the experiments with smoked surfaces and crackled glazes which she had begun previously. Meanwhile her range of imagery continued to expand. She describes the studio in Wandsworth as being "womb-like" and her own work at this epoch as being part of an often painful process of introspection. Writing about some of the work of this period, the art critic and potter Emmanuel Cooper spoke of what seemed to him its "curious passivity"[vii]. In fact, it seems more accurate to describe some of the pieces as having a kind of stillness and compressed energy.

vii   Emanuel Cooper, 'Glenys Barton – Sculptures and reliefs', *Ceramic Review*, No.85, 1984

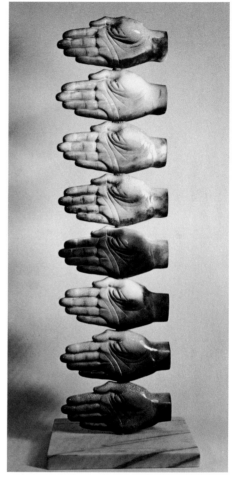

A Column of Hands

125 x 15 cms
Collection: City Museum and Art Gallery,
Stoke on Trent

RIGHT:
Hand

30 x 15 cms

Triangular Hands   1983

40 x 60 cms

Cooper's attention was particularly caught by the sculpture *Inside* 1983, a crouching female with bowed head and arms locked around her legs – "a figure almost without sex in which the mood is one of self-containment, [and] perhaps, introspection."[viii] In one of its aspects, the figure is a self-portrait, but the sculptor has smoothed away most of the particular details – the head, for example, is smoothly modelled, totally without hair, like all the figures and heads which Barton made at this period. The surface is unified with a raku glaze, sandblasted to reveal a fine network of crazing.

Other significant sculptures from this time include the *Lady with Three Faces* (1980), a piece of which Barton is still particularly fond; some self-portrait reliefs, showing the head full-face and in profile; and reliefs called *I Know* and *I Will Know*. In these latter, a profile head contains a crouching figure. Certain common themes emerge. *Lady with Three Faces* is fairly obviously a sculpture about being forced to make a choice between different identities, and the multiple aspects of the self-portrait reliefs seem to be a way of making a similar statement. The *I Know* reliefs can be read in several different ways – as allegories of a perhaps unwelcome knowledge of self which forces itself on the artist's consciousness, and also (this is especially true of *I Will Know*, where the contained form is foetus-like) as foreshadowing the birth of a child. The artist's son Felix was born in 1982.

viii Cooper, in ibid.

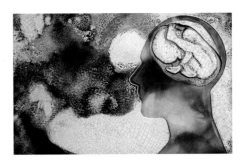

I Will Know   1981

25 x 40 x 3.4 cms

LEFT:
Inside   1983

From a series of 12
9.5 x 15 x 18 cms
Private Collections, UK

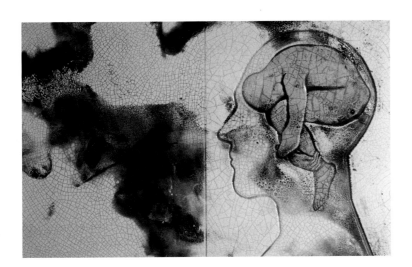

I Know   1981

25 x 40 x 3.4 cms

Self Portrait I 1981

22 x 30.5 x 3 cms

Self Portrait II 1981

22 x 30.5 x 3 cms

RIGHT:
Profile Head I 1986
66 cms high
Private Collection, UK

In 1984, Glenys Barton moved to Essex. Her new studio was the garage of the house she and her husband Martin Hunt bought at Creeksea, near Burnham-on-Crouch. The closed spaces of London were replaced by the immense open skies of the flat Essex coastline, where land and water intermingle, and her work took on a correspondingly greater feeling of openness.

A particularly significant development at this time was a return to making heads – life-size and sometimes larger. During her final period in London, Barton had made one female head, 9½ inches high – therefore somewhat less than life-size. This was based on the appearance of her close friend Jacqui Poncelet, but was not, she now thinks, a fully developed likeness, any more than were the self-portrait reliefs of the same period mentioned above. Now she tackled the problem of making a true portrait, a likeness of the art patron Peter Moores. Moores, with his compact, balding head and fine profile, already seemed linked in appearance to the heads she had been making hitherto. Barton began by making some large-scale profile drawings of him, then, in a complete break with her previous method of work, made a handbuilt, one-off sculpture, with no use of moulds. She sees this as being both a major step forward (her technical methods have been mixed ever since this moment, combining the use of moulds with hand-modelling as occasion and mood seem to demand), and as a reversion to her way of working as a very young woman, before she went to the Royal College of Art.

The way Moores looked impressed itself on Barton's imagination to the point where he became the inspiration for a series of works, including some profile heads – essentially reliefs without the background. Glenys Barton sees in these profiles the influence of Giacometti:

> I realise that I have been influenced by Giacometti's invention of forms for the human figure, for instance to take the flattening of the human head into an axe-like profile shape. I have not, however, been in any way influenced by his expressive style. My favourite Giacometti piece and therefore the one that has been the most influential is the small portrait he did of his mother in 1927 which is flattened from front to back.[ix]

It is nevertheless typical of Barton's development and in particular of her increasing tendency to oscillate between realism and idealisation that the series of Moores portraits should have been accompanied by another and

ix From the artist's notebooks, 14.2.92

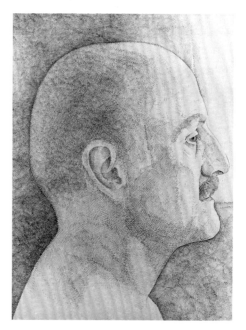

Peter Moores   1985

Ink on paper
99 x 74 cms

RIGHT:
Peter Moores   1990

58 cms high
Private Collection, UK

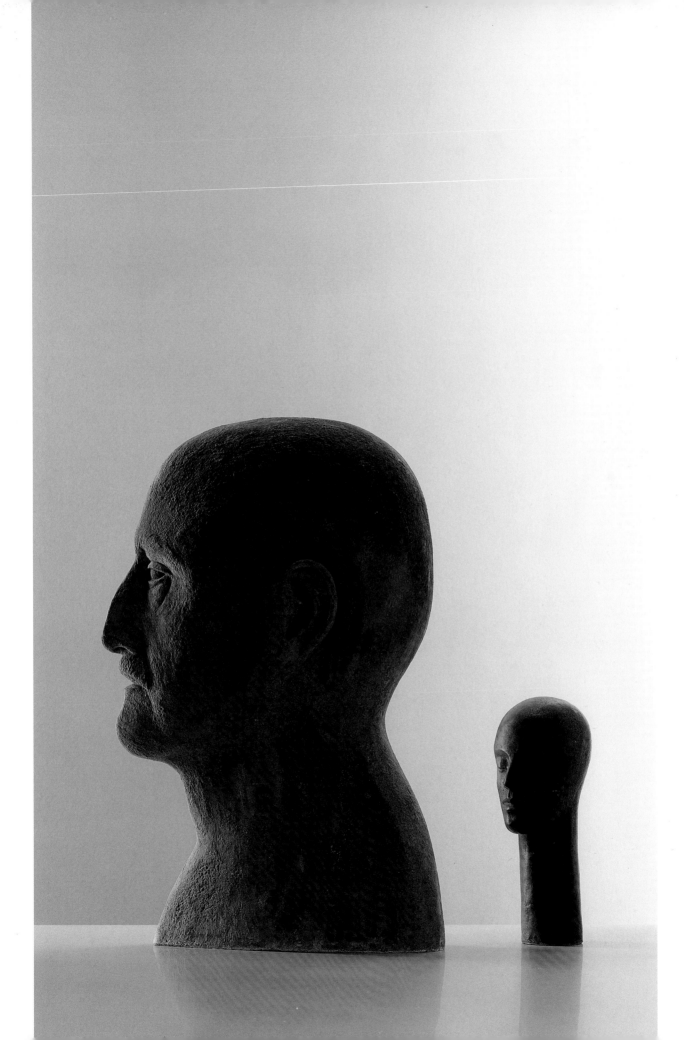

The Rite   1987

35 x 45 x 45 cms
Private Collection, UK

LEFT:
Green Madonna 4 (Lucy)   1987

 50 x 23 cms
Collection: Norwich Castle Museum

quite different one – Madonna heads inspired by Piero della Francesca's famous *Madonna del Parto*. Renaissance art was henceforth to have an ever stronger appeal for Barton's imagination – she strove to emulate its calm regularity and grandeur.

Yet a third series of heads, more idealised than those of Peter Moores but less so than the *Madonnas*, were based on the appearance of Jacqui Poncelet's husband, the sculptor Richard Deacon.

One feature shared by all three series is the fact that Barton used them as a basis for renewed experiments with both colour and texture. She glazed her heads blue, then sand-blasted the glaze in order to obtain a matt surface. Continual experimentation with colour and surface has in fact been one of the features of her work, from the late 1970s onward.

The garage at Creeksea was obviously inadequate as a permanent workspace, so a new permanent studio was built beside the house. In 1987, while she was waiting to move into the new space, Barton's concern – and often anxiety – about the actual scale of her work reached one of its periodic moments of climax. She experimented with a large head covered with ceramic mosaic, and also with a grouping of kneeling figures, *The Rite*, where the component parts, arranged in a circle, create a sculptural environment. These attempts to work on a larger scale continued after the new studio was ready for occupation. The first piece she made there was a large self-portrait with a mask, where the material was not her customary ceramic, but fibreglass. She soon gave up these attempts, however, both because she disliked the medium, which is in any case very unpleasant to use, and also because she felt that these larger pieces in some mysterious way became "invisible". Later she wrote in a notebook:

> A question of scale. When does one recognise that the
> scale of the work is right? At what point can this
> become a lack of challenge? Rightness or complacency?
> I think I have found the right material and scale in
> which to express myself. Now I have to expand or
> consolidate my ideas to reach that ideal expression of
> the human spirit.[x]

Her occupation of her new workspace was accompanied by other important changes in the rhythm of her life. For example, she finally gave up teaching. The major advantage was it gave her more time to work, and meant an absence of interruption. Yet there were disadvantages as well.

x   From ibid., 23.2.92

Self Portrait with Mask   1987

155 cms high

RIGHT:
Richard IV   1986

48 cms high
Private Collection, USA

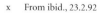

While, for example, she now had more time to study, she was cut off from the resources of the library at Camberwell. Because of this, she began to collect illustrated books on art in a much more serious and systematic way, as references for her work. Living a much more reclusive life, her true companions, as she now says "were early 20th century artists from my books: Cézanne, Matisse, Picasso, Modigliani, Giacometti."

Reclusiveness was balanced by occasional extended trips abroad – to Thailand in 1990 and to India in 1995. Both these trips had an important impact on her work. The Hindu sculpture she saw in Thailand reinforced her interest in multifaced imagery, particularly images of the god Brahma, and she was also impressed by the centred calm of the Buddhist sculpture she saw. In India she looked at Jain sculpture, and visited both Hindu and Buddhist sites – Ranakpur, Ajanta, Benares and the great temple at Khajuraho, with its teeming erotic figures.

LEFT & BELOW LEFT:
Multi-faced Head I   1990

28 x 20 x 25 cms
Private Collection, UK

BELOW RIGHT:
Multi-faced Head II   1990

31 x 20 x 27 cms
Private Collection, UK

Her work from the late 1980s onwards shows much greater variety and is also a great deal freer in conception. As previously, however, one can make a broad distinction between works which are realistic in impulse and works which are idealising. Amongst the most poetic of the idealising sculptures are those in which the idea of the multiple head or face is developed in three dimensions. Barton's notes on this subject are suggestive. One runs in part:

> An approach –
> Make a form and then add faces – see what happens.
> The faces may change the form or not. As people move
> within crowds and within relationships to fit in with
> each other, so could the parts of the sculpture.[xi]

Another reads as follows:

> While working on a multi-faced piece.
> Sometimes the form takes over: – considerations of
> form take first place. Sometimes the faces [subject] take
> over... Letting things 'just happen' is very difficult for
> me. I am not that kind of person but I am getting better
> at it. [xii]

xi   From ibid., April 1992
xii From ibid., 15.9.92

BELOW & RIGHT:
Facing   1995

33 x 52 x 33 cms

Untitled 1992 & Untitled 1993

26 x 26 x 22 cms/26 x 29 x 22 cms

On the Inside   1996

48 x 63 x 58 cms

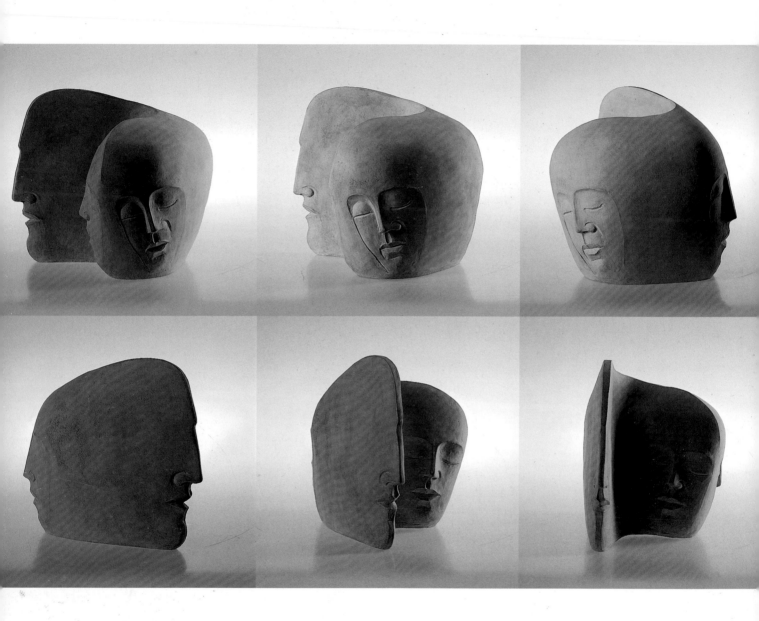

Dreaming Edge   1994

28 x 30.5 cms

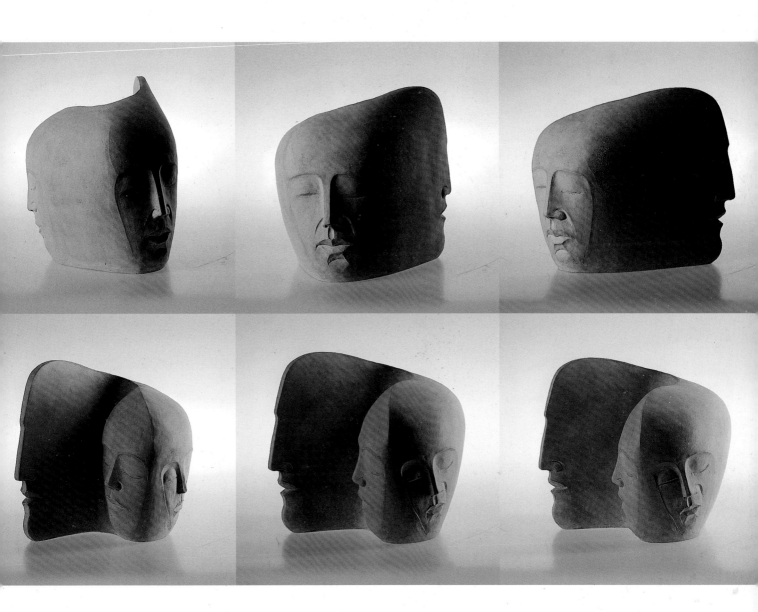

The multi-faced pieces do in fact demonstrate a clear development both towards something more integrated and towards something which is more clearly organic in form. Gradually separated shapes become one shape. Heads which would have been treated in full relief are now raised from the matrix so subtly that it is difficult to distinguish between passages of fully rounded modelling, passages which are in very shallow relief, and other passages which are simply drawn upon the surface in sgraffito. One especially fascinating aspect of these works is that they absolutely demand that the viewer move round them – there is no one standpoint where they can be seen complete. Very often, too, the spectator is required to come closer, and actually look downward and into them. This is the case, for instance, with two pieces of 1995, *Facing* and *Inside Edge*. Each of these consists of two separate curved forms, placed so as to face one another. Overlapping visages appear on the inside curve of each form – there are details which can never be seen completely if one stands at a distance from the sculpture.

One striking characteristic of these sculptures is their fluidity and their relationship to the idea of time. Barton's early work makes use of rigid, sharply defined forms. Here the aesthetic is quite different. Though the heads offer sharp, crisp profiles – the frontier where the form ends – within the boundary things melt and slide into one another. The eye reads the relationships first one way, then another, and both readings are equally valid.

Similarly, in early work one is often conscious of the sculptor's fascination with the idea of the remote past. *Ozymandias*, with its direct reference to Old Kingdom sculpture, is a good example of this. But there is never a suggestion that time, so to speak, is still flowing through the sculpture itself. The moment is frozen. The opposite is the case with recent sculptures featuring multiple faces or heads. The spectator's own movement around the piece seems to trigger this flow – the sculptures are kinetic in a peculiarly personal and subtle way.

In strong contrast to these 'idealising' pieces is Glenys Barton's production as a portraitist. In an age when good portraiture of any kind is increasingly rare, and when good portraiture in three dimensions is especially so, she has been carving out an important place for herself in this difficult field. The portraits of Peter Moores which have already been discussed in this essay are transitional. His appearance was, by happenstance, already closely linked to the work which Glenys Barton was then producing. The new series of portraits represents a breakthrough into a rather different way of looking at things. Many of them, though not all, represent women, and Barton has had to invent new ways of getting a likeness. Her intelligent plundering of the past has obviously played an important role in this. Her own list of influences includes things as different from one another as Tudor portraits, Etruscan figures seen in the museum at Barcelona, early Iberian art, and the work of Cézanne, Modigliani and Picasso.

The earliest of this new series of portraits are those of the couturier, the late Jean Muir. Muir's spare, pared down aesthetic was obviously very sympathetic to the artist. So too was her personality, as expressed in her characteristic stance and gestures as well as in her style of dress. In most of the portraits Barton includes Muir's hands. The bust is extended to accommodate this. There are also some full-length statuettes, which make the most of Muir's slenderness, and her raised shoulder pose, at once contemplative and slightly sardonic.

What makes these pieces so extraordinarily telling is the way in which Barton has simplified appearances, keeping only things she found telling and significant. She seems to have learned this technique of simplification from ancient art, Etruscan terracottas in particular. Compared with the vast majority of contemporary portrait sculpture, the Jean Muir portraits have extraordinary spontaneity and freshness. They also have traces of a popular accent. It is perhaps not straining things too far to find in them, and especially in the small full-lengths, references to nineteenth century Staffordshire pottery figures.

Jean Muir   1992

67 x 13 x 3 cms

Through her portraits of Jean Muir Glenys Barton came into contact with the National Portrait Gallery. The 20th century curator, Robin Gibson, immediately appreciated the quality of her work, and Barton was commissioned to make a portrait of another celebrated female personality, the Member of Parliament and former actress Glenda Jackson. In some ways this was a far more problematic enterprise than the portraits of Jean Muir, since Jackson is notoriously uninterested in and unselfconscious about her own appearance. Asking for photographs to work from, for instance, the sculptor found that Miss Jackson had kept none from her time in the theatre. Nevertheless Barton had such vivid memories of her subject's performance as Gudrun, in the film of D.H. Lawrence's 'Women in Love', that she decided to combine an image taken from the film with one of Glenda Jackson as she is now. The result was an extension of the theme of the multiple head.

In other portraits from this time Barton restudied people whose appearances she has used before, in a more remote and stylised fashion. She made a naturalistic portrait, for example, of Jacqui Poncelet. This too incorporates the sitter's arms and hands.

One of the things which Barton had to do, when embarking on a much broader range of portraits, was to find ways of dealing with things she had hitherto managed to avoid. A particular problem was hair, in particular the coiffures of her female subjects. Hitherto Barton had always avoided representing this – hair does not generally form a compact mass; the strands move and shift and the whole surface constantly changes its form. The process of learning what to do was gradual. Neither Muir's neat geometric cut, nor Glenda Jackson's hair, which she now keeps short, presented insuperable problems. Since then, the sculptor has gradually learned to deal with coiffures less immediately amenable to her methods – like the fringe in *Amanda I* (p.96), a portrait of the painter Amanda Faulkner. This, in turn seems to have led to increased freedom of handling which embraces other details as well. *Nick and Megan I* and *II* (p.104/105) are near half-length sculptures inspired by the Italian Renaissance, Bellini and Botticelli Madonnas in particular. The forms are subtly flattened – what looks fully three-dimensional exists chiefly in very subtle low relief. Barton has become more and more adept at manipulating the spectator's perception of depth, and she uses this skill to surround the form with a quivering atmospheric envelope.

RIGHT:
Glenda with Hand   1993

51 x 46.5 cms

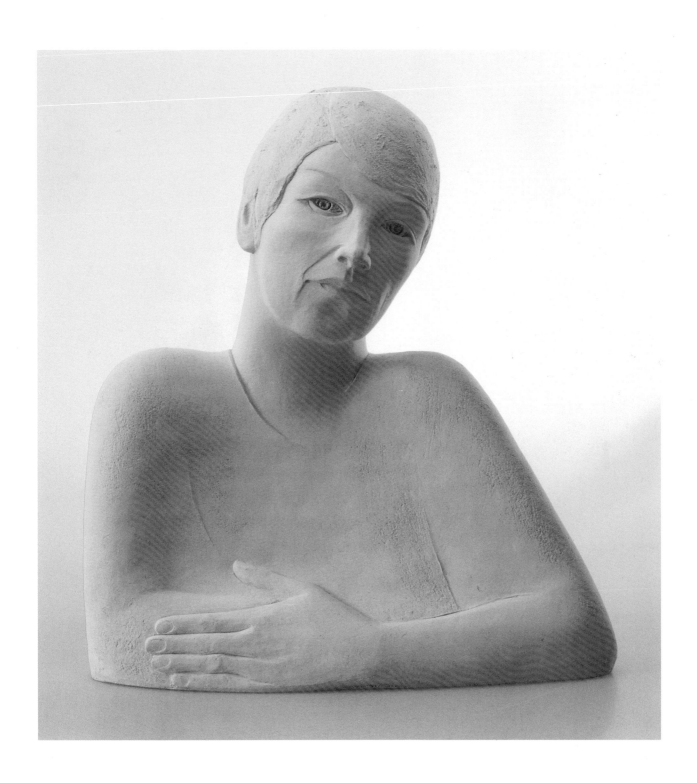

In addition to making portraits of people she knows and has actually seen (though she also makes extensive use of photographs when actually creating a portrait) Barton has made some of people whom she does not know personally – of her heroes, the great artists of the Modern Movement. Her primary source for these seems to have been the photographic portraits included in a book of my own, 'Lives of the Great Twentieth Century Artists'. Among the artists whom she has depicted, using this source, are Mondrian and Umberto Boccioni. The portraits are much simpler and less specific than those of still living subjects. *Mondrian*, with his bald head, is perhaps related to the likenesses of Peter Moores, but the approach is more direct. *Boccioni*, with eyes incised rather than modelled, is an apparition rather than a portrait in any conventional sense of the term. These 'likenesses' express the enormous respect which Glenys Barton feels for these great predecessors, her reverent feelings for what they were able to accomplish.

Another source of inspiration in recent years has been details from great Renaissance frescos. The illustrations she finds in books of seminal Renaissance masterpieces like Masaccio's frescos in the Brancacci Chapel in Florence encourage her to approach this material in a peculiarly modern fashion. These illustrations enable and indeed encourage the spectator to focus on isolated details, where the audience in a pre-photographic age would clearly have read the compositions in a different way. The heads singled out by the camera, and often reproduced nearly full scale in major publications on Renaissance art, have already undergone an initial process of simplification. The dry, chalky tones of fresco also have an affinity with matt ceramic surfaces. There is another, subtler link as well to the things that Glenys Barton now does. Masaccio and his immediate followers in Florence, and Piero della Francesca in Umbria, were especially fascinated by the problem of expressing volume through the use of colour and line on a flat surface. Barton, too, continually juggles with our perceptions of volume and depth.

Boccioni I   1989

43 x 25 x 10 cms
Private Collection, USA

LEFT:
Dreaming II   1996

42 x 45 x 26 cms
Private Collection, USA

The idealistic spirit, always so strong in her work, does not confine itself to the contemplation of the universe of art. In a recent letter to me she says:

> Although directly political work does not usually interest me, underlying everything I do is a deep concern for our survival both socially and environmentally. I listen to Radio 4 current affairs programmes every day as I work. [xiii]

Examples of this concern are Barton's *Green Warriors*, a variant on the medieval theme of the Green Man, which appears in medieval church carving (particularly in capitals and roof bosses). This image also interested Elisabeth Frink who made a number of *Green Man* heads towards the end of her life.

In Frink's case the Green Man symbolised a personal hope of recovery from illness. In Barton's the references are different. When she was in Thailand in 1990 she was impressed not only by the Hindu and Buddhist sculptures she saw, but by the pollution in Bangkok and by the devastated condition of some rural parts of the country. When she returned home this devastation was matched by the damage done by a gale to her own home at Creeksea. Her studio has been damaged, and a number of trees blown down. The *Green Warriors* are an act of mourning for the latter, and also an emblem of hope, of faith in the power of nature to regenerate itself.

xiii Letter to the author, dated 3. 2. 97

RIGHT:
Green Warrior I   1990

49 x 24 x 27 cms

ABOVE LEFT:
Small Green Warrior 1990

38 cms high

ABOVE RIGHT:
Still Green Warrior 1990

47 cms high

RIGHT:
Green Warrior I (Back) 1990

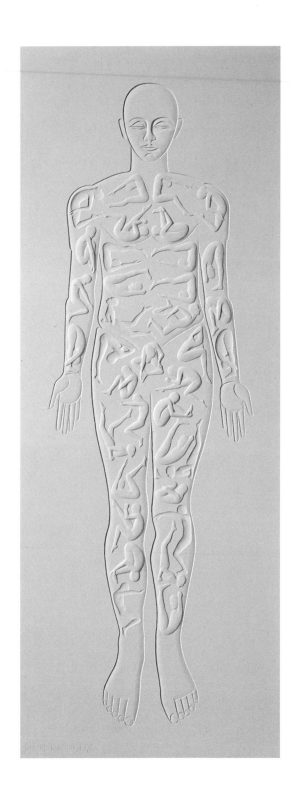

The work Barton is engaged on now reflects her social and environmental concerns more directly than ever. She speaks of her feelings "about the encapsulation of society within itself and the individual being indivisible from his surroundings"[xiv]. At the moment of writing, the initial expression of this is a large drawing – a single figure, in a pose reminiscent of Jain sculptures, contains many other figures. Barton sees this design as emblematic of her anger and frustration over what happened to British society in the 1980s. It is also surely much more than this. Almost from the beginning of her career the figure or head containing another figure has been a leitmotif, and it is not surprising to find her returning to a variant at this moment in her career. It is part of her vision of things that she continually searches for some kind of inner or hidden truth.

It is also part of her artistic make-up to experiment with new ways of doing things. She is now, for example, speculating about computers, and looking for ways of using them in her work.

Barton will never, despite this, be an artist who is committed to a mechanistic view of things. Nor is she a sculptor whose concerns are essentially formal, concerned with making shapes and creating relationships between forms. She cares passionately about the state of the world, and her sculptures are essentially the product of this concern. On the one hand she feels that the solitary individual can do little to ameliorate a situation she sees as one which is steadily worsening, both sociologically and ecologically. On the other, she feels a duty to attempt to do something. However, she also feels something else: that, since she is an artist, the effort must primarily be made through her art. Many artists, when they become campaigners, separate this activity from what they actually make. This is not the case with Glenys Barton. In fact, the idea of an artist who campaigns is probably repugnant to her.

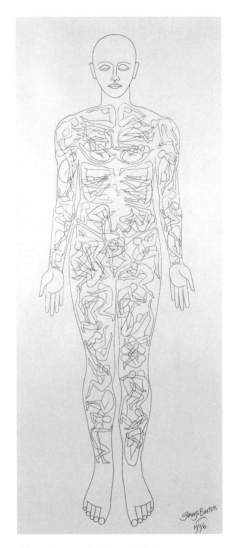

There is no such thing   1996

Pencil on paper
150 x 68.5 cms

LEFT:
There is no such thing   1996

Plaster
155 x 64 x 42 cms

xiv   ibid.

57

One reason why the religious art of Jainism, Buddhism and Hinduism appeals to her so strongly is clearly that she herself has a meditative temperament. Her idealised heads and figures, in particular, are objects for contemplation. Still more so are the recent multi-headed and multi-visaged sculptures, where the features often seem to melt into the basic form that contains them, then rise up from it again.

BELOW & RIGHT
Dreaming III   1996

Terracotta
48 x 55 30 cms
Private Collection, Saudi Arabia

Inside Out IV   1996

30.5 x 24 x 28 cms
Private Collection, UK

OVERLEAF FROM LEFT TO RIGHT

Profile Head II

66 cms high
Private Collection, UK

Richard IV

Richard I

Pink Madonna

This contemplative bent is balanced by a lively response to other human beings – the primary reason why she has recently enjoyed so much success as a portraitist. One feature of her portraits is their informality. They have all the freshness of a completely spontaneous response – something which is much more often met in drawn or painted portraits than in sculpture. This response is linked to the material she uses. While she has on occasion complained that being a sculptor in ceramic, rather than in supposedly 'nobler' materials, such as stone or bronze, she is aware, not least from long familiarity with it, that clay responds with almost unique sensitivity to the maker's hand. Today her concern as a technician is to find a balance between the wide variety of processes which ceramic permits. It can be moulded so as to give a crisp, almost rigid result. Or it can be modelled with complete freedom and spontaneity. Something which adds to this freedom is the fact that it also offers a surface both for incised lines – that is, for a kind of drawing – and, through the use of glaze, for colour. Its textural variety is almost infinite.

In one sense, Barton stands somewhat apart from recent developments in sculpture. She is not a practitioner of *arte povera*, making art from discarded elements found in the environment. Similarly, she is not a maker of environmental, scenographic works which surround and enfold the viewer. She makes precisely designed, finite objects, and these objects, in turn, are the product of laborious technical processes which impose their own rules and sequences of action. Every maker of ceramic objects knows what disasters can take place in the kiln if these rules and sequences are not followed. Though ceramic is, as I have said, a material which invites spontaneity, it is also one where the development of that spontaneity is brought to a halt at a certain point by the nature of the technical process. Once the piece is fired, it is very difficult to have a change of heart and make radical alterations.

Another reason why Barton's work stands apart is that she is obstinately figurative, and this figuration is not 'found', but created *ab initio*. For her, as for the sculptors of the past, the human image can be used to encompass all the many meanings she finds within herself. Her sculptures offer a continual dialogue – they ask questions about what it is to be alive in this particular epoch. And they often leave room for more than one answer. This is why I, like many people who have come into contact with them, find them fascinating and moving.

GLENYS BARTON'S PORTRAITS
by Robin Gibson

Portrait sculpture has always been something of a poor relation to
portrait painting. Scarcely considered worth a nod in most books about
portraiture, its derivation from funerary monuments and its associations
with architecture, mostly of the mausoleum genus, have by and large
rendered it beyond the reach of popular and domestic taste. Piers Gough's
recently redisplayed Nineteenth Century Galleries at the National Portrait
Gallery are an outstanding example of imaginative exploitation of the
traditional connotations. Serried ranks of busts in deathly white marble
or black painted plaster, both monumental and commemorative, are
deployed to provide an appropriate architectural and philosophical
framework for an imperial hall of fame, a concept characteristic of the
High Victorian approach to the Gallery's collections.

In an earlier era, sculptors of the baroque and rococo had succeeded in
bringing extraordinary levels of movement to the human figure and
unprecedented realism to drapes and costumes. It was, however, during
the era of High Victorian classicism that Rodin finally gave life to the
sculptured figure and portrait bust. Creating convincing translations of
living bodies and individual personalities from wet clay, he set standards
which have been built on by Epstein and others, but never surpassed.
Marcel Tirel remembered the extraordinary physical, almost erotic,
lengths to which Rodin went to achieve the immediacy of life in portraits
of his model, Claire Coudert, Duchesse de Choiseuil: '[she] lay down on
the floor on her back, her head turned towards the light, her neck held
firmly between his knees, while he modelled with his thumb, first
touching her flesh and then the clay, his thumb still warm, so to speak,
from her skin!' (M. Tirel, *The Last Years of Rodin*, London, 1928).

Rodin was more or less contemporaneous with the revolution in painting
brought about by the impressionists and their successors. This
spontaneity in the approach to human likeness broke the classical
deadlock which had held sculpture in its grip since the Renaissance. The
discovery that there were other traditions in sculpture from Africa,
Oceania and earlier civilisations provided the final impetus for the
unleashing of sculptural trends in every direction, Picasso to cubism and
beyond, Brancusi to abstraction. While British sculptors like Gill, Dobson
and Lambert capitalised on the stylistic and decorative possibilities

LEFT:
Jean Muir   1991

52.5 x 33 x 16 cms
Private Collection, Paris

opened up by cubism and Brancusi, only Epstein (and possibly Gaudier-Brzeska, had he lived) were big enough to master all the implications of the new freedoms. The apparent dichotomy in Epstein's work between the formal innovations of his monumental work and the Rodinesque modelling and expressivity of his commissioned portraits, however, remained unresolved to the end and set a trend which continues even in the work of contemporary sculptors like William Pye and Angela Conner.

On the continent, artists sought different solutions to the problem of working with the human figure and physiognomy. Coming via surrealism, Giacometti pared away Rodinesque modelling in a never-ending search for the essence of personality as an aesthetic entity in time and space, and arrived at a symbol for the existentialist mood of his age. In Italy, Marino Marini, one of Glenys Barton's few twentieth century predecessors to have worked specifically in clay and colour, sought a new classicism via the works of the Etruscans and created tragi-heroic figures on horseback and elegiac portraits with a different sort of defiant pathos. The late Elisabeth Frink's work sometimes touches on that of middle period Marini, though the aggressive masculinity of her figures can appear clumsy and her portraits bland in comparison to those of Marini, with his gift for evolutionary form and the grace and gravity of his modelling.

Today, 'contemporary sculpture' has become an almost meaningless term, encompassing anything from room installations to piles of pigment, the remains of dead beasts in formaldehyde and, most regrettably of all, life-size heads, inexpertly modelled in clay and cast in bronze – an undead craft masquerading as portraiture, for which, in the age of virtual reality, there can be few excuses. Where, in the midst of the current conceptualistic free-for-all known as contemporary art, can we place the ceramic figures and, for the purposes of this essay, the portraits of Glenys Barton? With some justification, they appear difficult to pigeonhole, a hybrid from sources as various as the artist's own background, but quietly demanding our attention with a unique presence and integrity. It is Barton's consistency of approach and the underlying humanism in her work which ultimately enabled her to tackle portraiture, qualities she shares in common with several distinguished and ultimately unclassifiable contemporary painters such as Lucian Freud and Maggi Hambling, for whom portraiture was also a gradually achieved response to evolving personal and artistic concerns.

RIGHT:
Female Head 1981

26 x 14 x 20 cms
Private Collection, UK

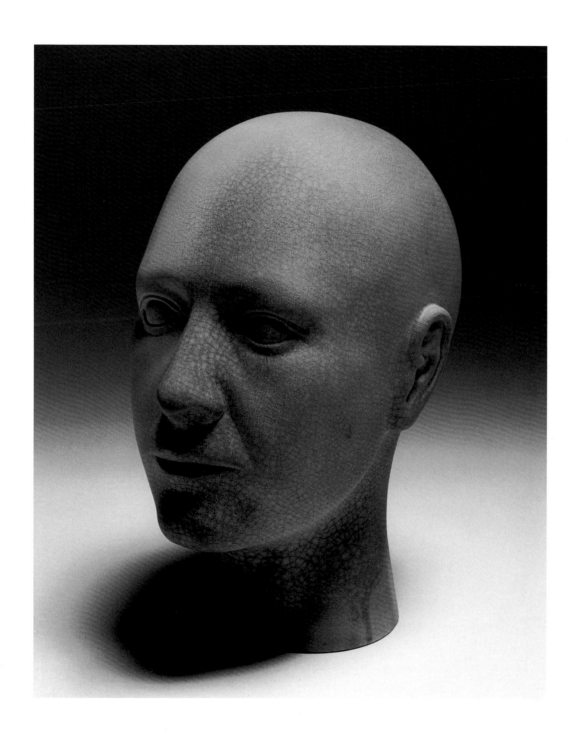

The self-portrait is a discipline often chosen by young artists as a means of self-examination at a time of insecurity, – doubts about the face which they must present to the world and the direction which they and their art intend to take. It is therefore somehow reassuring that Barton also felt compelled at the beginning of the eighties to undertake this exercise, thereby producing her earliest portrait work. The first of these was *Lady with Three Faces* (1980). A small standing figure in bone china (the material a legacy of her residency at Wedgwood), it reminds us immediately that at one point Barton would have liked to have been a dancer. The relationship between sculpture and the dance is well known. With Barton, the figure at once suggests that it is the poise, the self-control and the grace which are significant for her. These attributes might well be seen as one of the more specifically feminine aspects of the dance and are in stark contrast to the masculine athleticism of some of Marini's work. For the rest, the little naked figure, a potent symbol for Barton's persona, establishes the silent calm characteristic of much of her mature work, a characteristic which is not necessarily in itself an attribute either of sculpture or of the ceramic medium. Rather than a frenzy of self-examination at a moment of crisis, the figure radiates an aura of tranquillity and waiting, waiting for the right moment in the choreography of life when she will, in full knowledge of what she is doing, stoop to lift up one of the three faces which have been positioned ready on the stage for her.

The small series of *Self-Portrait* plaques from 1981 are a continuation of the same theme: a Janus head in high (or low) relief looking in three directions, a mask, if you like, from which the artist, still in undefined and unseeing profile, will select the right way to go forward. The elaborate craquelure in the monochrome glaze is at once decorative and at the same time suggestive of the web of contradictions and imperfections which impede this choice. It also imperceptibly ensnares the small crouched figure *Inside* (1983), another self-portrait motif, which at first sight may seem to be an image of despair but in reality is more like a coiled spring, waiting to leap into life when the cue is given.

Barton's work of the seventies and early eighties tends to concentrate on the figure, often positioned Giacometti-like in a loosely defined space or in an environment, though the idea of doing a portrait *per se* was not in itself new when she accepted the commission for a portrait of Peter Moores. A series of *Female Head*(s) in 1981 had been based in a general sort of way on her long-standing friend and fellow ceramicist, Jacqui

Lady with Three Faces   1980

43.2 cms high

Poncelet, and exhibit the same sort of essential simplicity as the figure work and self-portraits of the time. The *Peter Moores* portrait, the idea for which came from Barton's participation in the 1981 Peter Moores Liverpool Project 'Art into the Eighties' exhibition, was, however, a more specific challenge and Barton began by producing the extremely painstaking but monumental drawings to which she only rarely resorts, soon after moving studios in 1984. Almost architectural in their precision and grandiosity, such drawings are invariably connected to a monumental piece in which the traditionally spontaneous use of the ceramic medium cannot be left to chance.

The large *Peter Moores* portrait, at least twice the height of previous heads, is indeed memorably monumental. Both its size and the green coloration with the rough texture of ancient weathered bronze suggest an archaic, early classical model, heightened by the use of the flattened profile which is centred on Moores's 'roman' nose. The transformation of a mustachioed Liverpool businessman into ancient warrior would appear to have all the ingredients and pitfalls of operatic farce, but Barton's vision and seriousness of purpose produce an image of great integrity, with a thoughtful aloofness of character and a masculinity far superior to its Victorian equivalent – the white marble politician in a toga.

Concurrent with the *Peter Moores* were not only some other profile heads but also the sleeping madonnas, heads with closed eyes, originally a reference to the traditional downward look of modesty seen in paintings and sculptures of madonna and child. One might speculate that Barton had so far evaded the difficulty of representing eyes in sculpture and that this was yet another solution to the problem (a similar problem would again present itself in years to come with subjects who habitually wore glasses). Eyes, traditionally the mirror of the soul, are also the point at which the portrait confronts the viewer and demands recognition as a living entity. To date, Barton's sculptures had been objects of contemplation, even including to a large degree, the portrait of Peter Moores. Suddenly, and perhaps where least expected, the 'sleeping heads' begin this process of confrontation. The closed eyes already imply a physical condition, sleep or even death, and a greater realism in Barton's modelling, a consequence perhaps of working on the *Peter Moores*, emphasises the link between the object and life.

LEFT:
Sleeping Madonna   1986

42 cms high
Private Collection

On a par with the sleeping madonnas is a portrait of Jacqui Poncelet which was soon followed by its pair, the *Richard III* of Poncelet's husband, the sculptor Richard Deacon, both dating from 1985. Both heads are fully modelled and appear to be sleeping, sharing the melancholy which is characteristic of Barton's work at this time. Whereas the wife is placid, peaceful, little different perhaps from the 1981 *Female Head*, the portrait of *Richard*, slightly open-mouthed, seems more restless – to the extent of emitting an almost audible sigh. Both heads are sandblasted white, the pallor of sleep. In the sleeping madonnas the colour, which has become an increasingly significant element in Barton's work, is equally instrumental in evoking a mood of restless sleep. The heads are dappled with soft shades of green, mauve and blue onto white, reminiscent of shadows cast by moonlight falling through the gently moving branches of a tree beyond an open bedroom window.

The succession of heads of Deacon which followed *Richard III* during 1986 mark a significant transformation in Barton's work. Not only do the eyes at last confront us, but Deacon's chiselled features and upright bearing seem to have engendered a new, physically vigorous phase in the sculpture which is almost specifically masculine. Adrian Flowers's remarkable photograph of *Richard IV* shows a virile sculptural form thrusting upwards to the sky, the slightly truculent expression suggesting a reserve of masculine aggression, with the highly sculptural protruding ears a further potent symbol of an active physical presence. The green bronze coloration of this and others in the *Richard* series and the smooth, rather schematic modelling of the features again seem to refer to bronzes of Greek or Etruscan warriors; though these are not to be confused with the *Green Warriors* which appeared several years later and are specifically symbolic, pacifist and ecological heads covered with organic growth, the vanquished perhaps rather than victors.

How far the heads of *Richard* are portraits in a conventional sense is open to question, one on which those who know him better than the writer can comment. A comparison with Marini's terracotta portrait heads of the 1940s such as those of *Ulrich* and *Manuel Gasser* shows that not only, with their air of battered archeological finds, are Marini's heads more specifically Etruscan in character, they are also fully modelled portraits in which Marini uses the roughness of the clay to indicate expression and individual features, and the warmth of earth pigments to suggest realistic local colour. Barton's portrait heads of the eighties in comparison are unashamedly idealised, their archaic references employed both for purely

Jacqui & Richard   1985/86

Ceramic
41 x 38 cms

RIGHT:
Green Madonna I & II   1987

38 cms (I)
35 cms (II)

formal reasons and to create a mood, rather than simply as a stylistic solution to the problem of creating a portrait in the ceramic medium. It is probably more accurate to view the heads as sculptures inspired by a particular individual rather than as attempts at an accurate representation.

The series of male heads which appeared over the next three years is seen to great effect grouped in Adrian Flowers's photograph on the back cover of the catalogue of Barton's 'Artists and Green Warriors' exhibition at Flowers East in June 1990. Even the central, highly stylised terracotta head, ostensibly of an Ingresque woman, has an androgynous energy which is totally in keeping with the overriding virility of the others. Very noticeable in this photograph too is the flattened perspective employed for nearly every portrait and head from *Richard IV* onward. Sometimes described by Barton as 'high relief', the formal thrust of the pieces is nevertheless fully three-dimensional, the ears protruding almost like thumbs from the fist-like form and supplying both balance and movement.

The preoccupation with ears evident here found its ultimate expression in several named portraits of artists which Barton based on photographs she had found in Edward Lucie-Smith's 'Lives of the Modern Artists'. Significantly, they are of influential figures, Boccioni and Duchamp, who had both experimented with new ways of expression, Boccioni in particular with sculpture. The actual physical relationship between the resulting heads and either the work or the appearance of the artist in question is perhaps tenuous. For Barton, it was more an act of homage to two great creators in which, by adopting the features of their faces, she could work out her current preoccupations. All these heads are quite severely flattened, like masks on standing forms perhaps, but despite acute stylisation of features and colouring they exhibit an intelligence and alertness which is largely due to the ears and eyes. As with the Deacon heads, the exaggerated ears are not only formally significant but more importantly suggest a state of 'listening'. The *Duchamp* (1989) is serene, knowing, with a half-smile, and finished in a rough-patinated bronze colour which itself suggests maturity. The eyes are incised in formal arabesques which echo similar figurations in the ears. *Boccioni I* and *II* both use a more rounded head form, a shape from which the regular features and the slightly staring almond-shaped eyes appear almost to have been cut out. The tension and note of inquiry implicit in the first

PREVIOUS PAGE LEFT:
Richard VIII   1987

50 cms high

Boccioni II   1989

41cms high

RIGHT:
Duchamp   1988

42 x 25 x 11 cms
Private Collection, UK

head are heightened in the second by deeper moulding of the features and further breaking up of the patchy blue-on-white coloration, the result being a raw and rather primitive creation of some power.

An opportunity for greater naturalism presented itself when Barton decided to do a portrait of her opthalmologist, John Grindle, a man whose appearance she not only knew well but which seemed to fit in with some of the preoccupations shown in recent heads. *The Norman*

BELOW FROM FRONT TO REAR

Boccioni II 41 cms high

Cloud Man I 47 cms high

Boccioni I 43 cms high

Cloud Man II 45 cms high

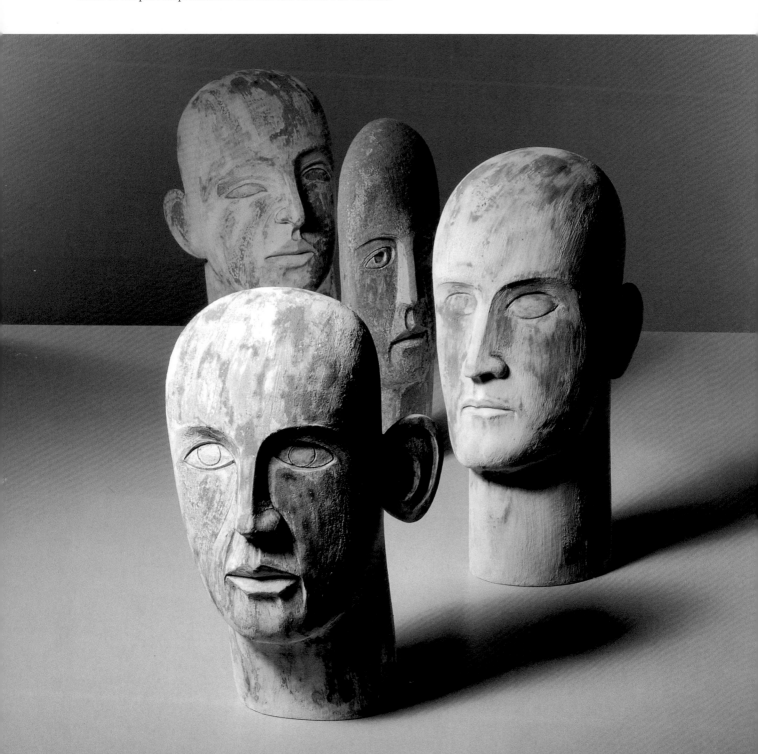

Opthalmologist (1989) is appropriately a 'seeing' rather than a 'listening' head, and the smallish and realistically formed ears are held back against the immaculately contained and upright form. Indeed, smoothness is of the essence here, both literal and metaphorical, a fact which the gentle irony of the title (an allusion to the sitter's ancestors) serves to underline. A luminous turquoise glaze covers rather languid but perfect features, bringing light and movement to the portrait. The perfectly incised and almond-shaped eyes stare somewhat lazily but comprehendingly at a point beyond our reach. For the first time, there is the suggestion of an immaculate haircut. The strangely angled but by no means obvious flattening of the head enlivens a number of viewpoints and again contrives to emphasise the mood of sophistication. This is the head of a man we feel we would recognise, a likeness in a more conventional sense, but seen as we were intended to see him, through the eyes of the artist.

These indications of a willingness to grapple with the particularities of an individual likeness scarcely prepare us for the *tour de force* of the sculptures of the late Jean Muir, which were begun in 1991. Not only the appearance of the distinguished fashion designer, but indeed her creative personality pervades the resulting pieces to the extent of dictating their form, colour and mood. Undertaken at Barton's request, drawings prepared the way for the first piece, a wonderfully graceful figure which enabled her to formulate her ideas for the more direct portraits which followed. The figure already exploits Muir's distinctive features, the hairstyle, the characteristic gesture of the hand raised to the face and the supremely elegant cut of the simple long dress. Left uncoloured, the figure has the mute elegance and poise of a tanagra statuette.

The route chosen from statuette to portrait bust is not altogether clear, especially as the bust format was without precedent in Barton's oeuvre. The solution in *Jean Muir I* of cutting the figure off at the elbows, and folding the left arm across the bottom of the piece to grasp the right elbow, not only creates a base for the sculpture and another gesture characteristic of the sitter, but above all establishes a compact pose in which the inner tension of the piece is made explicit, both sculpturally and psychologically. Colour and definition are now brought into play. The dark blue pigment used for all areas except the flesh is, of course, derived from the sitter's preference for the colour but also adds dignity and weight to the portrait. Less predictably, it is also used to delineate Muir's features strongly, brilliantly evoking her make-up, but also, particularly in the eyes (which have been changed from those of the figure), to engage slightly

The Norman Opthalmologist   1990

46 x 24 x 12 cms
Private Collection, UK

Jean Muir II   1992

52.5 x 33 x 16 cms

RIGHT:
Jean Muir   1992

67 x 13 x 3 cms

obliquely, but none the less intensely, with the viewer. The simple head now in the Scottish National Portrait Gallery repeats this formula, but in an even more intense and compact columnar form.

Barton was not yet finished with the bust format, however. *Jean Muir III* is a virtual repetition of the original, which had sold rapidly to a private collection in France. Its loss deprived her of the inspiration of its undoubtedly successful approach to a number of problems. *Jean Muir II*, however, embodied a subtly different approach, which, apart from the obvious difference in colour and the elegant and relaxed placement of the hands, created a very different effect from the sombre confrontation of *Jean Muir I*. Serene in white, the rich opalescent glaze sandblasted to a smooth dryness on the face and hands, Muir's expression, achieved by moving the position of the eyes, is now one of calm and elegant thoughtfulness. Like many of Barton's earlier works, it reverts to being an object of beauty for quiet contemplation and retains all the timeless elegance of the original statuette.

Concurrent with the *Jean Muirs* were two projects, both of which share concerns in common with the portrait of the fashion designer. The faceless *Two Boys* (1991) was based on a snapshot of Barton's son Felix and a friend, and clearly uses the portrait to solve a problem in three-dimensional composition and the sculptural fusion into satisfactory form of two figures. Coincidentally, the solution is not dissimilar to Marini's early terracotta *People* of 1929, though there the figures are cut off at the waist. For Barton, still thinking about Jean Muir, the disposition of the hands and the pervasive blue colour were clearly significant, and the result is a touching image of friendship. There is some reminiscence, too, of the tranquil elegance of the blue and rose period paintings of Picasso, to whom Barton had been paying particular attention at this time.

When asked to provide a nude for a Flowers exhibition on this theme, Barton turned to Picasso's likeness for a nude bust, self-evidently based partly on the early cubist self-portraits of 1906 and partly on late photographs of the master working shirtless in his studio or playing on the beach. Titled *The Man Himself*, the bust combines the intensity of the earlier artists' heads (and ears) with a rather traditional, if bulkily cubist solution to the naked torso, though it is perhaps less successful in achieving a satisfactory fusion between the two.

Jean Muir Portrait Head   1992

46 x 19 x 12 cms
Collection: Scottish National Portrait Gallery

LEFT:
Two Boys   1991

56 x 56 x 12.5 cms
Private collection, USA

Staying with the portrait bust, Barton returned to the device she had used in *Jean Muir I* – using the hand to support the head. In *Mum*, a portrait of her mother, made in connection with another Flowers themed exhibition, 'Portrait of the Artist's Mother Done From Memory' (1992). It is a recognisably vivid image of maternal weariness, which successfully adopts the traditional solution of the pyramid shape for its form. With the head resting on the hand and the eyes closed either in intense concentration or overwhelming tiredness, it has a slightly histrionic quality which Barton has not as yet attempted again.

All these works show a willingness to experiment and seek new solutions and directions. Barton's recent study of Picasso now bore fruit in the *Axe Head* and *Janus* series of the next few years, both of which make use, at least in part, of his so-called 'two-faced' and multiple perspective paintings of heads. *Matt and Huei* (1992), a portrait of Matthew Flowers

The Man Himself (Picasso) 1991

63 x 53 x 22 cms

RIGHT:
Mum 1992

45 x 38 x 13 cms

84

and his recently married wife, was the first portrait as such to combine two heads in one graceful form. In this piece, Huei is seen in exquisitely proportioned full face and flanked by the narrow axe-like profile of her husband, both faces contained within the one form and by the enveloping blue of the *Jean Muir*. The sculpture is an irresistible metaphor for male and female, day and night, sun and moon, where the movement of the viewer or of the light may suddenly cause the one to eclipse the other.

LEFT:
The Dreamer   1992

25 x 28 x 23 cms

Matt and Huei   1992

28 x 33 x 24 cms
Private collection

When invited by the National Portrait Gallery in 1993 to undertake a portrait of Glenda Jackson, Barton was quick to realise how her sitter's dual roles as actress and politician could be exploited, using a different approach to the 'double-headed' piece. Working both from her own photographs and from film stills of Jackson as 'Gudrun', her Oscar-winning role in Ken Russell's 1970 film of 'Women in Love', Barton produced two versions of *Glenda and Gudrun*. Both versions are basically one-sided and meant to be viewed from in front. The first for the NPG has a solid, realistically modelled and coloured portrait head of the sitter, which is shadowed on the left, almost protectively, by the flattened *alter ego* of the film role. Wearing a hat and coat and modelled in low relief on a subtly smaller scale, the Gudrun emerges from behind and slightly above, the two persona bound together in a sculptural curve. In keeping with the trend towards greater realism in her portraits and in particular with the contrast here between the real person and the performer, Barton colours the 'Glenda' head in flesh tone, using brown for the hair and blue for the shadows, using relatively less colour for the 'Gudrun'. The effect is slightly disconcerting: both the formal relationship between the realism of the principal head and the artifice of the *alter ego*, and the rather cinematic contrast between the two, being so little expected in a sculpture. Its intentions are clear however and its validity as a Barton portrait, a 'bio-sculpture' perhaps, beyond doubt.

Interestingly, in *Glenda and Gudrun II* (which as the result of an accident no longer survives) the same principles failed to achieve such effective results, mostly perhaps because of the equal prominence allowed to both heads. The Gudrun head, this time in an all-over, nunnish head-dress from another scene in the film, was placed on the right, fully modelled and coloured in white, and somehow managed to rob the principal head of much of its presence. The same formula worked very well in the touching *With Me* pieces of the same period, but here, with the two simply placed next to and looking away from each other, the connection between them seems somewhat arbitrary, more like two different people who happen to be standing close to each other.

Barton subsequently returned to safer ground with *Glenda with Hand*. The half-length bust format in white in a sense repeats the tranquil elegance of *Jean Muir II*, while using a textured finish instead of the glaze for the clothes and hair. The crossed arms, ending in a finely modelled and extended hand, create the base for an asymmetrical pyramid, the head inclined and listening, the expression thoughtful and comprehending –

With Me II   1993

39 x 30 x 19 cms

RIGHT ABOVE:
Glenda and Gudrun I   1993

Collection: National Portrait Gallery

RIGHT BELOW :
Glenda and Gudrun II   1994

40 x 32 x 8 cms

ABOVE:
Large Janus   1993

38 x 50 x 20 cms
Collection: Manchester City Art Galleries

RIGHT:
Axe Head   1992

34 x 33 x 10 cms

Large Axe Head I   1993

61 x 50.5 x 15 cms
Private Collection, UK

LEFT:
With Me I   1992

35 x 27 x 18 cms

Jacqui I   1994

51.5 x 49 cms

Jacqui II   1994

54 x 37 cms

the perfect image of a sympathetic presence and keen intelligence, sitting on the other side of the table, communicating with the viewer.

A similar approach and finish were again employed for the *Jacqui I*, one of a large group of portraits which Barton completed in 1994. The head of Jacqui Poncelet, Barton's friend of long-standing, is inclined away from the viewer, with the hands folded, and a slightly concave curve given to the main body of the bust, which increases its grace. In *Jacqui II*, this curve is further exaggerated, the head raised and the hands clasped tightly under the chin, suggesting an alert involvement with the proceedings which is slightly reminiscent of the first *Jean Muir* bust. In the interests of increasing realism, however, the dress and distinctive little felt cap are coloured a greenish turquoise, and Poncelet is shown wearing her glasses.

The problem of what to do with spectacles on a portrait sculpture is an old one and had been preoccupying Barton for some time, especially since she wanted to make a head of Robert Heller, a Director of Angela Flowers Gallery, who was never seen without his glasses. Almost as a preliminary exercise, Barton returned to the heads of artists she had started in 1989 and selected the bespectacled Mondrian for her inspiration. The result is a thoughtful little head, treated, almost instinctively one might guess, in an angular fashion and with very little colour. The spectacles are modelled very much in low relief, their circular form contrasting with the almost straight lines of his features, the eyes glimpsed as indentations on the surface. Both *Mondrian* and the finished head of *Bob Heller* share something of the immediacy of a Marini portrait in their small scale and roughish finish, the *Bob Heller* in particular with its local colouring of flesh and indigo and his typical benign half-smile. In his case, the spectacles are treated a little more three-dimensionally, their modern outline coloured and lifted away from the right side of the face. *Jacqui II*, on the other hand, posed more of a problem. The heavy-rimmed butterfly shape of Poncelet's glasses in relation to the semi-profile pose left a far more substantial void between the right side of the face and the spectacle rim, which, of necessity could only be suggested by neutral colouring. This quest for realism and the resulting slightly goggle-like effect is a disconcertingly brave attempt, but in the end perhaps only serves to draw too much attention to the spectacles.

Dick Barnes   1994

56 x 56 x 15 cms

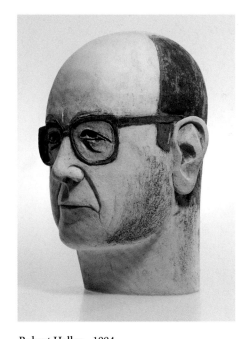

Robert Heller   1994

39 x 24 x 18 cms
Private Collection, UK

Further portrait busts for 1994 included the commissioned bust of Dick Barnes, husband of an American patron, and two of the artist, Amanda Faulkner. The *Dick Barnes* represents in a sense the culmination of Barton's pursuit of realism. Basically this is one of her pyramidal busts with arms in a highly relaxed and asymmetrical pose; Barnes is nevertheless fully kitted out, not only with spectacles, but also with jacket, shirt and graphically detailed hair, all fully coloured, including a new yellowish green for the jacket and for some of the shading (achieved by a thin wash of the blue used elsewhere on the piece). The roughish finish acts as a counterfoil to the detail and local colour. With some reminiscences of *Mum*, but with a far more lively sense of engagement, it is an ambitious piece in a thoroughly traditional portrait format – which works in its own idiosyncratic way.

Amanda I is also a highly successful and communicative piece, though in a rather different way, which includes a number of stylistic innovations. The pyramid form is squeezed and softened into the continuously flowing curves of the asymmetrically sloping shoulders, creating across the front of the body a hollow curve of the left arm and hands, which echoes the simple round neck-line of the dress. All obtrusive shapes, with the exception of the elegantly modelled nose, are softened, and the hands, eyes, ears and fringe are calligraphically incised into the surface of the clay. The blue colouration is equally handled with great simplicity and sophistication; the shading round the eyes and touch of colour on the lips suggesting depth and contour in the otherwise shallow modelling, rather than any form of make-up. Barton's willingness to manipulate the ingredients of the portrait material in front of her into a purely sculptural solution are (to my mind) invariably more successful than when she seems to be more preoccupied with the minutiae of the individual likeness. Not that there is any loss of verisimilitude in *Amanda I*. Indeed it has a sense of recognisability, and more importantly, of intimacy which elevate what to all intents and purposes is a less spectacular piece to one of her most convincing portraits. *Amanda II*, unfinished and unglazed at the time of writing, returns to a more regular pyramidal bust form, but the head is now fully turned to one side to capitalise, as it were, on Faulkner's profile and neatly bobbed hair.

Amanda I 1995

56 x 41 x 15 cms

Working on several versions of a particular piece at once is part of the creative methodology of modern art; the sense is of working towards a solution and producing series rather than creating individual set pieces. In Barton's case it often provides a link between most of her portraits and the rest of her work. This is particularly noticeable in the heads of film-maker John Tchalenko and his son Luke where the *Luke* heads reflect similar concerns to small, very three-dimensional pieces like *Dreaming Edge* of the same period (1994). The three heads of Luke were inspired by his long flowing hair and by his face – with its perhaps slightly Egyptian look (at least, as it appears in Barton's sculpture). One can see how the *Lukes* and some of the *Dreaming* pieces are sculpted, not only fully in the round, but actually out of the round, Luke's hair being the form by which the head is both enclosed and at the same time projected. These call to mind not only the rounded forms of the heads of Egyptian mummy sarcophagi, but also, especially in the *Lukes II* and *III*, some of Henry

LEFT:
Amanda II   1995

56.5 x 55 x 18 cms

Luke II & III   1994

Each 29.4 x 29.4 cms

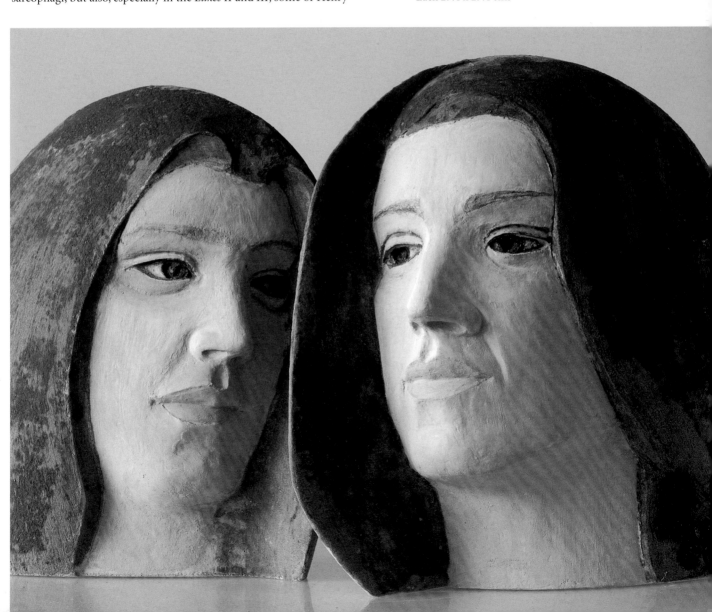

Moore's *Helmet Heads* or Epstein's little early head of Romilly John, the hair somehow being the sculptural form which both encloses and discloses the unique personality within. The one-off head of *John*, which was done after those of *Luke*, is based on a much earlier photo of the sitter with long 1970s hair; though more conventional both in form and with a rich blue overall glaze like *Luke I*, it should be seen firmly in the context of the *Luke* series. It shares, of course, the same formal concerns, but also records Barton's discovery through the medium of her work of family features common to both father and son.

Luke I 1994

31.8 x 30.6 cms

While working on further 'dreaming' and double or multiple-headed pieces through 1995, Barton was nevertheless planning several ambitious portraits which suggest that, for the past couple of years at any rate, portraiture had become the dominating force behind her work, though perhaps this was inevitable with the forthcoming exhibition at the National Portrait Gallery in mind. Significantly, four of the six new subjects are family and friends, chosen one suspects, not only because of their familiarity, but also because of the freedom these subjects would allow in experimenting with new formats. The first of these *Nick and Megan*, exists in two versions and is of a neighbour and her new baby. The concept is self-evidently a return to the recurring theme of the Madonna in Barton's work, but for the first time an attempt to tackle it *in toto* as Madonna and Child. Both *I* and *II* are extended half-lengths to below the waist, a new feature which is common to nearly all the new portraits; both show the mother cradling the child in her arms, her head inclined, looking down at the baby. No.*I* in blue is the more compact piece, flattened and modelled in quite low relief, the baby sleeping with his head on the mother's shoulder, back to the viewer, only the mother's right elbow extended to break the otherwise symmetrical outline of the sculpture. No.*II*, coloured in palest wash, suggests, unjustifiably perhaps, the passage of a month or so since the first piece. The baby seems larger and is now leaning back over his mother's protruding right arm, staring at the viewer (as babies do) and demanding recognition as an independent being. In fact, the baby has seized the focus of our attention. If *Nick and Megan I* is a more or less traditional image of maternity, no.*II* which also seems to outline Megan's features, hairstyle and ample figure with greater individuality, is far more like certain cinquecento images of the Madonna and Child, where the baby's characterisation already indicates that he is the principal player on the scene.

Maternity in a personal sense is also evident in the portrait of *Felix*, Barton's son, shown half-seated like a small chinese mandarin (he is not placid enough for a bhudda). The incurved format of the figure echoes not only his wide-legged pose but harks back to the similar concave compositional device in *Jacqui II* of two years earlier. The pale-featured head (which also exists in an independent, more contemplative monochrome version) is resolutely turned away, a gesture which seems to suggest all the solemnity and truculence of early adolescence. Barton's husband *Martin* did not escape her attention at this time, but proved far more difficult for reasons she cannot satisfactorily explain. Using a rather

Dreaming Edge I   1994

28 x 30.5 cms

RIGHT:
Felix   1996

75 x 49 x 37 cms

Nick and Megan I   1996   Nick and Megan II   1996

67 x 53 x 15 cms   75 x 62 x 15.5 cms

solid version of the quarter-length bust format – which in itself suggests a certain comfortable passivity, it captures something of his good looks and open friendliness, but both physically and psychologically misses out on his tallness and nervous energy.

The sort of psychological detachment which may well be necessary for a successful portrait came much more naturally with Barton's next commission for a portrait of Lisa Miller, wife of collector Tim Miller. A practising counsellor and used to sitting and listening, the sitter herself clearly provided much of the detached objectivity which is evident in Barton's quite naturalistic portrait. This is another extended half-length; the crossed knee of the sitting position is here brought forward to provide the base for the otherwise slightly flattened figure. The pose, one feels, is as characteristic of the sitter as is her relaxed but alert expression. The naturalism is heightened by the skillfully shaded wash of colour over the simple blouse and skirt and the warm realism of the flesh tone. On more than one level, it feels like a highly sympathetic likeness.

RIGHT:
Lisa Miller   1996/97

73 x 46 x 22 cms
Private Collection, UK

Martin   1996/97

61 x 51 x 21 cms

The same could be said of the portrait of *Carole*, also executed in 1996, though the contrast could hardly be greater. A standing three-quarter length, it is perhaps Barton's first portrait since the statuette of Jean Muir to suggest height and poise in the figure. It is also the first – in the coquettishly inclined head, self-conscious pose and contrasting black and white patterns of the elaborate dress – to suggest movement and even fun. Characteristic of the sitter as these features undoubtedly are, the vertical format and the drama of the reddish blonde hair and patterned costume nevertheless demonstrate the full possibilities of ceramic and polychrome sculpture in a way which is markedly more extrovert than most of Barton's work to date. The artistic preoccupations found in *Carole* find their echo in Barton's most recent project, for a portrait of the distinguished barrister, Helena Kennedy, whom she has long admired. Barton's interest in and involvement with her sitters is invariably a motivating force behind her portraits, even if, as she says, like Francis Bacon, she could not bear to have her sitter around while she is working. Sittings therefore are confined to meetings and some photographs. Work is in progress at the time of writing, but three extended half-length figures, one sitting and two standing, suggest through striking gestures of the hands that it is the lawyer's eloquence and vivacity which are Barton's subject.

The striking developments shown in these recent portraits and the constant search for new modes of expression in what to some might seem a rather limited medium is not only a cause for wonderment, but a reflection of the wholehearted involvement which Barton brings to all aspects of her creative output. Barton is intensely sociable. Since the *Jean Muir* portraits she seems to have found the contact that portraiture allows between her work and other people to be an almost irresistible stimulus. For her, portraiture not only now seems to provide the drive behind her work, but helps to retain the essential humanism at its heart.

LEFT:
Carole   1996/7

86 x 44 x 15 cms

Helena Kennedy III　1996/97

68 x 41 x 12 cms

Helena Kennedy II　1996/97

68 x 41 x 13 cms

LEFT:
Helena Kennedy I　1996/97

68 x 41 x 17 cms

OVERLEAF:
Green Madonna II　1987

35 x 18 x 20 cms

BIOGRAPHY

1935   Born, Stoke on Trent
1968/71 Royal College of Art

ONE PERSON EXHIBITIONS

1973   *Bone China by Glenys Barton and Jacqui
        Poncelet*, Waterloo Place Gallery, London
        Keramiske Bytteklodster, Museum of Decorative
        Art, Copenhagen
        Precise Forms in Ceramic, Oxford Gallery, Oxford
1974   *Sculpture and Drawings*,
        Angela Flowers Gallery, London
1976   *Sculpture and Drawings*, Galerie Het Kapelhuis,
        Amersfoort, Holland
        Sculpture and Drawings, Germeenttelijkmuseum
        Leeuwarden, Holland
1977   *Glenys Barton at Wedgwood*, Crafts Council
        Gallery, Waterloo Place, London:- An exhibition
        of 26 pieces of sculpture produced at the Josiah
        Wedgwood Factory, Barlaston, Stoke on Trent,
        over a period of 18 months commencing January
        1976. Subsequently shown privately with
        Wedgwood in New York in January 1978
1981   *Sculpture and Reliefs*,
        Angela Flowers Gallery, London
1983   *Sculpture and Reliefs*,
        Angela Flowers Gallery, London
1986   *Heads – Sculpture and Drawings*,
        Angela Flowers Gallery, London
1990   *Artists and Green Warriors*, Flowers East, London
1993   Flowers East at London Fields
1994   *Portraits*, Angela Flowers Gallery, London
1996   Flowers East at London Fields, London
1997   *Glenys Barton Portraits*,
        National Portrait Gallery, London
        Dreaming Edge, Manchester City Art Gallery,
        Manchester
        Glenys Barton, Flowers East, London
1998   City Museum and Art Gallery, Stoke on Trent

SELECTED GROUP EXHIBITIONS

1980   *Images of Man*, Women Artists, ICA, London
Arts   Council touring exhibition
        Sculptures in Clay, Yorkshire Sculpture Park
        British 20th Century Ceramics, Christopher
        Wood Gallery
1980/81 *Nudes*, Angela Flowers Gallery, London
1981   *Peter Moores Liverpool Project 6: Art into the
        Eighties*, Walker Art Gallery, Liverpool and
        Fruitmarket Gallery, Edinburgh
1982   *A Taste of British Art Today*, CAS Exhibition,
        Brussels
        Work by Gallery Artists 1980/82, Angela Flowers
        Gallery, London
        South Bank Show, Arts Council
1983   *Small is Beautiful: Part 3*, Angela Flowers Gallery,
        London
1985   *Black and White*, Angela Flowers Gallery, London
        Small is Beautiful: Part 4, Angela Flowers Gallery,
        London
1986   *Sixteen Years, Sixteen Artists*, Angela Flowers
        Gallery, London
        Multiplemedia, The Nicholson Gallery,
        Edinburgh
1987   *16 Artists – Process & Product*, Turnpike Gallery,
        Leigh, Greater Manchester
1988   *Contemporary Portraits*, Flowers East, London
        Figure II Naked, Aberystwyth Arts Centre
        and touring
        The Face, The Arkansas Arts Centre, Little Rock,
        Arkansas
        Out of Clay, Manchester City Art Gallery,
        Manchester
        Small is Beautiful: Part 6, Flowers East, London
1989   *Angela Flowers Gallery 1990*, Barbican Centre,
        London
        Badge Art II, Flowers East, London
1990   *Contemporary Portraits*, Flowers East, London
        Colours of the Earth, British Council touring
        exhibition of India and Malaysia
        Small is Beautiful: Part 8, The Figure, Flowers
        East, London

1991   *Art for Amnesty*
        Angela Flowers Gallery 1991, Flowers East,
        London
        Nudes, Watermans Art Centre, Brentford
        Four Heads, Northern Centre for Contemporary
        Arts, Sunderland
1992   *Artist's Choice*, Flowers East, London
        Small is Beautiful: Part 10, Animals, Flowers East,
        London
        *Portrait of the Artist's Mother Done From
        Memory*, Flowers East, London
1993/94 *The Portrait Now*, National Portrait Gallery,
        London
1995   *Contemporary Sculpture*, Collyer Bristow,
        London
        The Twenty Fifth Anniversary Exhibition, Flowers
        East at London Fields, London
        Flowers at Koplin, Koplin Gallery, Los Angeles
        Breaking the Mould, Methods and Materials of
        Sculpture, National Portrait Gallery, London
1996   Angela Flowers Gallery, Ireland
        Hot Off The Press – Ceramics and Print, Tillie
        House, City Museum and Art Gallery, Carlisle
        and tour
1997   Gwenda Jay Gallery, Los Angeles

PUBLIC COLLECTIONS

Abbott Hall Gallery
Boymans Museum, Rotterdam
Birmingham Museum
City Museum and Art Gallery, Stoke on Trent
Craft Council Collection, London
Contemporary Arts Society Collection
Leeds Museum and Art Gallery
Leicester Museum and Art Gallery
Manchester Museum and Art Gallery
National Museum of Victoria, Melbourne
National Portrait Gallery, London
Norwich Castle Museum
Pennsylvania State University Museum of Modern Art
Portsmouth Museum and Art Gallery

Princesshoff Museum, Leeuwarden
Reading Museum and Art Gallery
Royal Scottish Museum, Edinburgh
Scottish National Portrait Gallery, Edinburgh
Southampton Museum
Stockholm Museum
Stoke on Trent Museum and Art Gallery
Victoria and Albert Museum, London
Wedgwood Museum, Barlaston, Stoke on Trent
Welsh Arts Council Collection

BIBLIOGRAPHY

1972   *International Ceramics,* Victoria and Albert
        Museum, catalogue
1973   *The Craftsman's Art*, Victoria and Albert
        Museum, catalogue.
        Aspects of Modern British Crafts, Royal Scottish
        Museum, catalogue.
        Elizabeth Benn, Craftsman's Art, *Daily Telegraph,*
        (22 April)
        David Hamilton, Fine Art Ceramics, *Studio
        International*
        Tom Ferguson, What's happening, *Sunday
        Telegraph* (April)
        John Catleugh, *Ceramic Review No. 22*
        Jonn, *Politiken* (22 May)
        Mobilia No. 215 (June)
        Decorative Art in Modern Interiors. 1972-3,
        1973-4, 1974-5 Studio Vista
1974   Edward Lucie-Smith, *Ceramic Sculpture,*
        Oxford Gallery, catalogue introduction
        Lewenstein & Cooper, *New Ceramics,*
        Studio Vista
        David Hamilton, *Manual of Pottery and
        Ceramics,* Thames and Hudson
        James Heard, Angela Flowers exhibition, *Arts
        Review* (Nov.)
        Ceramic Forms, C.A.C. and British Council
        Ceramic Forms, Art and Artists (Dec.)
        The 2nd Chunichi International Exhibition of
        Ceramic Art, catalogue

Michael Robinson, *New Ceramics,* catalogue introduction, Ulster Museum

1975 Edward Lucie-Smith, The World of the Makers, Angela Flowers Gallery exhibition, Paddington Press

Elizabeth Fritsch, Angela Flowers Gallery exhibition, *Crafts* (Jan/Feb.)

Val Barry, Angela Flowers Gallery exhibition, *Ceramic Review No. 31*

John Catleugh, Off Centre, *Ceramic Review No. 31*

Michael Robinson, Modern Sculptors in Clay, *The Antique Collector* (Feb.)

The Artist, A Search for Order, *Ceramic Review No. 34*

1976 Fiona Adamczewski, Glenys Barton, *Arts Review* (Dec.)

The Artist, Down Mexico Way, *Crafts No. 22*

1977 Edward Lucie-Smith and John Mallet, Glenys Barton at Wedgwood, catalogue introduction

John Gainsborough, Glenys Barton, *Arts Review* (May and June)

Elizabeth Benn, Art moves in on the pottery floor, *Daily Telegraph* (June 18)

Collector's Guide, *Antique Dealer* (June)

Column, *The Times* (June 25)

London Day by Day, *Daily Telegraph* (June 15)

Edward Lucie-Smith, London Art Review, *Evening Standard* (June 16)

Peter Sen, *Daily Mirror* (June 15)

Edward Lucie-Smith, In View, *Art and Artists*

Sarah Kent, Review of Glenys Barton at Wedgwood, *Time Out* (July 8)

Artist Potter at Wedgwood, *Antique Collector* (July)

Elizabeth Benn, Antiques for the 2030's, *Homes and Gardens* (September)

Stephen Bayley, Glenys Barton at Wedgwood, *Crafts* (July/August)

Edward Lucie-Smith and John Mallett, Glenys Barton at Wedgwood, *Ceramics Monthly* (Oct.)

1978 *State of Clay*, Sunderland Arts Centre, Catalogue

1979 Press View, *Ceramic Review* (Dec.)

1980 Charlotte F. Speight, *Hands in Clay*

Margaret Walters, Women's Images of Men, ICA, catalogue introduction

Cover, *Art Monthly*, *Women's Images of Men*, ICA,

Arthur McIntyre, *Australian Crafts*

Nudes, Angela Flowers Gallery, catalogue

1981 Edward Lucie-Smith, Glenys Barton at Angela Flowers Gallery, *Art International* (Mar/April)

John Russell-Taylor, Art into the Eighties catalogue in *Art and Artists*

Irene McManus, Rooms without a View, *The Guardian* (Dec. 4)

Marina Vaizey, The art of the alternative, *Sunday Times* (Dec)

John Russell-Taylor, Equality for Potters and Photographers, *The Times* (Dec. 8)

British Ceramics and Textiles, Knokke Heist, catalogue

1982 Nancy Balfour, *A Taste of British Art Today* catalogue

1983 *New work by Glenys Barton*, Stoke on Trent City Museum and Art Gallery, catalogue

Charlotte F. Speight, *Images in Clay Sculpture,* Harper & Row, N.Y

1984 Emmanuel Cooper, Glenys Barton – Sculpture and Reliefs, *Ceramic Review 85*

1985 Sarah Kent and Jacqueline Morreau, *Womens Images of Men,* Writers and Readers

1986 Jane Cowe, Profile or Bust, *Arts Review* (May)

Giles Auty, Sponsored Walks, *The Spectator* (Oct 8)

Judith Bumpus, London and Regional Reports, *Art Line 30*

William Packer, Seductive beauty in pastel and glaze, *Financial Times* (Oct 23)

Emmanuel Cooper, Glenys Barton – Heads, *Ceramic Review 102*

1987 *16 Artists process and Product*, catalogue

1988 Mary Rose Beaumont, *Figure II – Naked,* catalogue

Townsend Wolfe, *The Face*, The Arkansas Arts Centre, catalogue

Edward Lucie-Smith, Flowers picks the best of the bunch, *The Independent* (Sept. 24)

Sarah Kent, Opening Show – Flowers East, *Time Out* (Sept. 28)

1989   Paul Rice and Christopher Gowing, *British Studio Ceramics*, Barrie & Jenkins

Eamonn McCabe on Karen Norquay, *Weekend Guardian* (Mar. 11)

Tim Kirby, Gone to Pieces, *The World of Interiors*, (May)

1990   *Artists and Green Warriors*, Flowers East, catalogue

Olive Watson, *British Studio Pottery*, V & A Publication

Emmanuel Cooper, Artists and Green Warriors, Crafts, (Nov./Dec.)

Tiffany Daneff, Private views behind the gallery, *The Sunday Telegraph,* (Nov. 25)

1991   *Art for Amnesty*, catalogue

Colours of the Earth, British Council, catalogue

1993   Robin Gibson, *The Portrait Now*, NPG, catalogue

Edward Lucie-Smith, *Glenys Barton – New Sculpture*, Flowers East, catalogue introduction

Guy Walters, Change of Image, *The Times Magazine,* (Nov. 20)

William Packer, Face Lift for the Portrait Gallery, *Financial Times,* (Nov. 19)

Clare Henry, The Arts, *The Herald,* (Nov. 20)

Tim Hilton, Farewell grandeur, hello fun, *Independent on Sunday,* (Nov. 21)

William Feaver, Faced with the famous, *The Observer,* (Nov. 21)

Brett Gorvy, Portrait Now, *Antique Collector* (Nov.)

Jose Manser, Practical Styling, *Design* (Nov.)

Ian R. Webb, A Classic For our Time, *The Times* (Nov.)

1995   Edward Lucie-Smith, *Art Today*, Phaidon

1996   The Telegraph Quiz, *Telegraph* (Jan. 15)

Susy Menks, Jean Muir, Building a Bridge between Art and Industry, *International Herald Tribune* (Jan. 10)

Charles Hall, Idols and Images, *Art Review* (Feb.)

Emmanuel Cooper, Glenys Barton – Portraits Today, *Ceramic Review 45* (Feb.)

Jean Muir Head in Scottish NPG, Home News, *The Herald* (Mar. 28)

Giselle Dye, About Face – an interview, *National Galleries of Scotland Newsletter* (May)

Pamela Kent, London Museums with New Displays, *New York Times* (Aug. 21)

Aileen Little, The Prime of Miss Jean Muir, *The Sunday Times, Scotland* (Oct. 3)

William Packer, Mutual recognition of talent, *Financial Times* (Weekend July 6-7)

Annabelle Auerbach, Arts Etcetera-The Sunday Picture, *Independent on Sunday* (Sept. 15)

Paul Scott and Terry Bennett, *Hot off the Press – Ceramics and Print*, Tullie House, Carlisle City Museum and Art Gallery, catalogue

1997   Jacqui Poncelet, *Ceramic Review, Sept/Oct*

Robin Gibson, Robert Heller, Edward Lucie-Smith, *Glenys Barton*, Momentum Publishing